About
Intercom

The way businesses talk to people online is broken. Intercom was founded in 2011 by Eoghan McCabe, Des Traynor, Ciaran Lee and David Barrett to fix it.

Intercom brings messaging products for sales, marketing and customer service to one platform, helping businesses avoid the stiff, spammy status quo and have real conversations that build real connections. Designed to feel like the messaging apps you use every day, Intercom lets you talk to consumers almost anywhere: inside your app, on your website, across social media and via email.

Today more than 17,000 businesses use Intercom to connect with a billion people worldwide. Our customers are some of the very best web and mobile businesses including Yahoo, Expensify, InVision, Hootsuite, New Relic, Product Hunt, Shopify and Hello Alfred.

Intercom has raised $116M in venture funding, and has 300 employees across its San Francisco headquarters, Dublin R&D office, and recently opened Chicago office.

Since Intercom was founded in 2011 we've published more than 500 articles on our blog Inside Intercom. Sharing lessons from our own startup journey has not only been the most fun for us to write, but also one of the most popular topics with our readership. This book compiles the most useful of those lessons into 9 questions that we believe every startup founder or early stage employee will find themselves asking at some point.

CAST OF CHARACTERS

Darragh Curran |
VP of Engineering

Sian Townsend |
*Director of Research
and Analytics*

Paul Adams |
VP of Product

Des Traynor |
*Co-Founder and Chief
Strategy Officer*

Bobby Pinero |
*Senior Director, Finance
and Analytics*

Eoghan McCabe |
*Co-Founder and
CEO*

Ben McRedmond |
*Senior Director
of Growth*

Matt Hodges |
*Senior Director of
Marketing*

Maggie Cohen |
*Director of
Recruitment*

Karen Church |
*Senior Manager of
Product Analytics*

Project Editor: *Geoffrey Keating*
Editors: *Jessica Shambora, Owen Williams*
Managing Editor: *John Collins*
Copy editing: *Adam Risman, Nathalie Marquez Courtney*
Design: *Intercom Brand Studio*

Additional contributors: *Emmet Connolly, Brian White, Kevin McNally, Nick Oldum*

Thanks to Mathilde Collin for writing such a thoughtful foreword.

For further information, contact team@intercom.com

ISBN 978-0-9861392-6-0

Foreword

By Mathilde Collin

―――――――

As a founder, it can feel like you always need more of something.
More users. More revenue. More engineers. More salespeople.
More funding. More time.

But there's one thing you can be sure you'll never run out of: advice.

Every startup has the luxury of learning from the mistakes and successes
of the ones that came before it, and the easy access we have to these
learnings is unprecedented. Experienced startup leaders generously
share their stories in the hopes of pushing the industry forward. From
company blogs, to tech news outlets, to online communities, to hardback
books, there is more publicly available advice on how to run a startup
than you could possibly digest. And that's not even counting what you
can learn from one-on-one meetings, small gatherings or events.

Advice from other founders, investors and tech leaders has been
invaluable to me in my career so far. Their stories and learnings have
helped me skip over hurdles where they stumbled and guided me through
my own obstacles along the way. Intercom itself has been a source of both
inspiration and concrete guidance: a company we aspire to be like that
shares its learnings with the world. A chat with the Intercom team about
SaaS pricing directly inspired the iterative strategy we use at Front today,

driven by getting as much feedback and data from customers as possible. Turning a startup into a success is famously difficult, and I think founders seek out so much guidance because they believe it will solve this problem (I certainly have). But it's important to remember that you have another incredible resource to draw from: your customers. As your company grows, what determines success is whether you build close relationships with your customers, understand their problems and solve them.

No one knows your customers, product, team and market like you do. You can build the most operationally sound company in the world, but if you're not building a product your customers want they'll find an alternative. Focus on your vision, talk to your customers, figure out what they need and build that.

The best content for growing startups doesn't prescribe what to do in inflexible terms. It gives examples of what's worked for other companies in their experience and gives you the tools to adapt those learnings for your business. That's the kind of advice I like to read and the kind of advice you'll find in this book.

Mathilde Collin is the CEO and co-founder of Front, the simplest way for teams to manage email.

Introduction

Our company, Intercom, is still a baby in most ways. Most things are not yet fully formed. Most things have yet to be "done". And yet it's not unfair to say at this stage that we have in fact "started up".

This book is a collection of the lessons we've learned over the past 6 years building our baby. We've written it for you, our customers and friends, and we hope you find it useful while building yours.

– Eoghan and Des, Intercom

CONTENTS ———

What will you build?

Foreword by Eoghan McCabe, Co-Founder and CEO

————

If you're trying to create a company that's successful, and you want to make something the market really wants and needs, do yourself a favor and build something you actually understand. Your startup will be approximately one trillion times more successful if you're solving a problem you've experienced yourself. And if you've experienced it, it's likely others have too.

When we started Intercom, we were solving a problem we had witnessed firsthand. Running our previous company, Exceptional, we knew so little about our users and their preferences. And there was no good tool to help us connect with them. We tried email, but it was impersonal and out of context. There was nothing out there that allowed an internet business like ours to maintain the same personal relationship with their customers the way, say, a coffee shop does with theirs.

So we built a small feature inside Exceptional that let us send a message to our users while they were in the product. It was pretty lightweight – a small JavaScript pop-up bubble – but our empathy for the problem led us to solve it in much more powerful ways. We couldn't have understood the nuances required to do so if we'd never had the problem ourselves.

Eoghan McCabe
@eoghan

Much <3 for @ciaran_lee and @davebarrett right now. They're building something very interesting...

6:50 PM - Mar 30 2011

Inventors and innovators can't help but become passionate about solving problems they experience, especially those that others aren't about to address. And passion is one of the most important ingredients when deciding what to build. When we started working on Intercom, we were just naturally excited about what you could use the technology to do.

This definitely wasn't the case for all the products we had built. Our previous company, Exceptional, was a developer tools company. It was successful, but we didn't care about it in the same way. A friend asked me rhetorically one day: "Do you wake up thinking of Ruby on Rails errors every day?" I remember being pretty offended at the time, but he was right. I did not wake up thinking about Rails errors. I had no passion for that.

Intercom is different and I think that's why we've succeeded so far. Our mission, and our product, has expanded over time, but we're still driven by pure passion about bringing businesses and their customers together, as people. No matter what you build, if you're really passionate about a certain problem, you'll almost certainly attract customers who are passionate about it too.

It's the question all startups begin with: What are we going to build? Founders agonize over their one big idea and how they're going to bring it into the world.

But the question of what to build is not one you can ever answer definitively. Even when you've released your product, it's being used by customers and you feel like you've got some traction, you still have to make hard decisions about what features to build next, what bugs to fix or what customer requests should be addressed. Sadly, none of us live in a world of unlimited resources, so there are always hard choices to make regardless of the stage your company is at.

PROBLEM FIRST, TECHNOLOGY SECOND

Let's start at the beginning. Before you make any further decisions, **make sure you're solving a real world problem**. One of the biggest mistakes founders make when developing new products is focusing on the technology itself, rather than what it will enable.

At Intercom we've found the Jobs-to-be-Done (JTBD) framework extremely useful in helping us stay laser focused on the problem. If you're unfamiliar with Jobs-to-be-Done, it's been popularized by Professor Clay Christensen from Harvard Business School and a good place to start is by searching for "Clay Christensen milkshake video".

In simple terms, JTBD says that people don't buy your product because of their demographic but because they want to hire it to do a job for them e.g. passing the time on a commute to work. That job has existed since the 19th century but whereas once newspapers were the most popular solution, now it's social media.

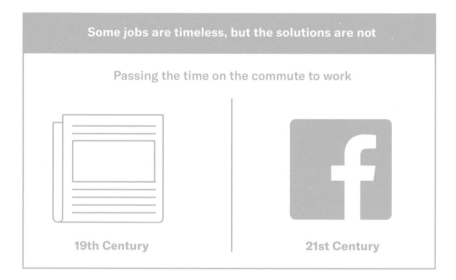

Using the lens of JTBD, it becomes apparent all technology flops have something in common. They failed to do a job for their customers. If you're struggling to identify a job your product does, proceed with caution. Technology that doesn't find a job fails.

The Segway, for example, was something people viewed as a technological advancement and therefore it had to be a great idea. It turns out it's not actually that useful to travel slightly faster than walking – but slightly slower than running – at a height about one and a half foot taller than most people. Unless you're a shopping mall security officer or a certain type of tourist.

As the author and designer Jim Kalbach has pointed out, innovations have two components, technological impact and market impact. Whenever you hear, "This is a breakthrough technology", the worry is you're in the top left quadrant and the technology is preceding the job.

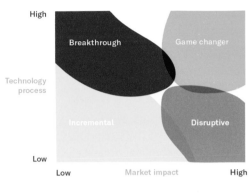

Credit: Jim Kalbach

It's arguable that's why Snap's Spectacles succeeded where Google Glass failed. Google Glass had to convince people who didn't wear glasses to wear glasses, while Spectacles are a new, cool pair of shades.

> **"It's much easier to tap into an existing behavior than it is to create an entirely new one."**
>
> – DES (CO-FOUNDER)

Truly disruptive products don't typically require a huge technological leap Instead, they usually just have a much better understanding of what the jobs to be done are. Take weather apps as an example. It turns out the reason customers hire weather products isn't for precipitation predictions, humidity estimates and 12-day forecasts. It's to answer far more primitive questions than that:

◊ Will it rain soon?
◊ Do I need to bring an umbrella?
◊ Should I have a barbecue tomorrow?
◊ Can I see what the weather forecast is
   without unlocking my phone?

CHANGING THE GAME

Of course, some products are simply game changers. That's when you unleash a new technology and present it along with real, useful things it can clearly do.

The original iPhone launch specifically focused on real things people needed to do, and showed how they were now possible in infinitely superior ways: listening to music, then finding a nearby Starbucks, calling them, placing an order and returning to music with guided navigation to your destination. There were no hypothetical use cases, e.g. "What if you could...", no aspirational "Wouldn't it be cool if..."

But be warned. It's often said that you can recognize a pioneer by the arrows in his back. The point being, first to market is often worst to market and breakthrough technologies don't often know how to explain what they've built. They'll talk about what it is, how it was built, what it's made of, etc. Broadly speaking none of that matters, and this is one of the reasons so many first movers fail. Competitors can sit back, observe the emergent use cases and deliver a product for them. So if you're launching a game changing technology make sure to clearly articulate the problems your product solves.

ANTICIPATE BUT DON'T FETISHIZE THE FUTURE

As founders and product people, you need to be acutely aware of all the different technological shifts happening in the industry and constantly ask yourself how these things will affect you. This is not some dry strategic exercise, just ask Garmin and TomTom. In 2007, satnavs were at the height of their popularity and then, somewhere in Moscone Center in San Francisco, someone waved an iPhone around on stage and their business was no more.

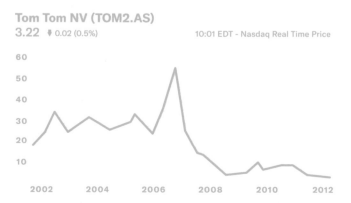

Garmin Ltd. GRMN
33.30 ↓ 0.13 (0.3%)   10:39 EDT - Nasdaq Real Time Price

The point is, it's not enough to just have a great product. You have to focus
on the technological landscape around you and what's coming down
the line, before it's too late. As former Intel CEO Andy Grove says, "Any
degree of success will breed complacency. Any degree of complacency
will breed failure. Therefore only the paranoid survive."

But there's a balance here. You need to be aware of the tectonic shifts
happening in your industry, but know which ones will impact your
product. There's a natural tendency for product people to fetishize the
future, but rather than enthusiastically latch onto the latest trends, it can
be better to take a step back and ask yourself – why?

There will always be emerging trends – artificial intelligence, virtual
reality, augmented reality, machine learning, conversational commerce –
all of which offer endless possibilities for your product. But you shouldn't
chase them just so you can ride a wave of hype. Fear of missing out, or
FOMO, is the motivating force behind large parts of what you see at the
Consumer Electronics Show or on Product Hunt, and many of these
products are searching for a quick exit of some sort.

So pay less attention to what's on the homepage of TechCrunch, and more
to the changes that are happening in the industry you're in. Technology
will continue to spit out one innovation after another. Whether it's
mobile, messaging or bots, the question you have to consistently ask

yourself is: Does this new technology make it cheaper, faster or easier for our customers to make progress in their lives? Because if it does make it cheaper, faster or easier for customers to make progress, and you haven't embraced it, you'll end up shipping v0.1 of yesterday's technology.

DO YOU NEED TO RE-INVENT THE WHEEL?

When considering what to build, most founders focus on what's shiny and new, forgetting that great products can be created by tinkering and improving on existing ideas, or by making unglamorous changes that don't require new technology.

By doubling down on what already works, you can focus on the first step where you can add value. For example, when Excel competitor Quattro Pro launched, they talked about how the product was better because it was written from scratch, rather than building features that *actually made it better* than Excel. It turns out people didn't really care how new their source code was.

> "Trying to be somebody else is a strategy doomed to fail. Don't deploy a bunch of tactics because that's what you think you're supposed to do. What works for someone else won't necessarily work for you. Imitation rarely achieves results."
>
> – EOGHAN (CO-FOUNDER)

Whether it's pattern libraries of UI, or older code that has been tested and fixed countless times before, they're not worse for having been used before. In fact they're better. Refining proven ideas adds clarity over time.

Of course there are times when you need to innovate, such as when existing patterns won't work, or what you're trying to achieve simply hasn't been done before. But if you've tried and tested ideas that work, build on them. Customers aren't paying for innovation; they're paying for a great product experience.

MAKE YOUR SOFTWARE MAGICAL

At its core, great product design is about cost-benefit analysis. How much does the user have to do versus the benefit they get in return? Whenever you find a way to dramatically reduce the cost – time and money – to the user and provide a greater benefit, you're creating something magical. Here are three ways the current generation of software feels magical.

1. The era of Uber-ification

We're in a new era of customer expectations. Long, messy processes are now unacceptable. Every user experience needs to be pared down to its minimal task.

The magic comes from using smart, context aware defaults, offering restricted choices and using single purpose screens to reduce your product to a single step. Today a single tap or swipe gets you a date, some flowers, a car, a movie, a restaurant and even a hotel. After that it'll get you a job, an apartment, a wedding and even a dog. David Sacks, founder of Yammer, described it as Uber-ification, and we seem to be approaching peak Uber-ification today.

David Sacks
@DavidSacks

Uber-ification = the slimming down of application interfaces into push-button experiences that do one thing. The next consumerization.

5:17 PM - Mar 12 2013

For business products Uber-ification isn't always immediately achievable. Most mature products must first unbundle into a set of single-purpose apps. Google's productivity tools (Gmail, Sheets, Docs, Hangouts, Drive) are the earliest example, but there will be more: large suites of software deconstructed into focused apps designed for specific jobs, all held together by a common identity system.

In short, if there's repeatable behavior in your product – checking in on a project, sending a message, ordering lunch or running a report – it should require nothing more than a couple of taps. The user's context – time, location, device, previous actions – combined with behavioral analytics and user preferences, can all be combined to offer a simple way to do complex tasks.

2. The end of data entry
Data entry is a fundamental component of software today, and it's clunky. Thankfully it's going away. The first improvement was the shift from recall to recognition. Rather than asking users to recall and enter items, you simply let them pick from options.

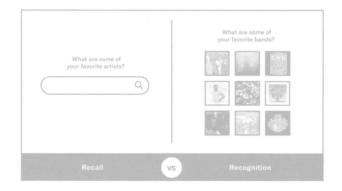

This is now the baseline of what we expect. The real magic comes from removing these steps entirely. Want to know who my friends are? Connect to my Facebook. Want to know who I work with? Use my email domain. The money I spend? Connect to my bank. The trips I've booked? You'll find the receipts in my email, like most things I've bought. With products like Gmail launching powerful APIs, the opportunities become endless.

3. Ambient awareness
Most of technology to date, all the way back to the written word, requires your full, undivided attention. It only works if you look directly at it. This is great for things like reading a book, but it's not so great for software products. Great software relies on ambient awareness – it conveys information without you looking directly at it.

Most of today's products are designed as destinations, places you go when you need certain pieces of information. But as much as living next door to a library doesn't make you a regular reader, having data on a reports tab in an analytics product doesn't make a user any smarter. The best products benefit customers with no action required on their part. Ask yourself, "How can I ensure that every user gets value from this product, even if they forget to log in?"

For your product this might mean push notifications, email digests, SMS alerts or daily reports to make sure that users are getting the full value of your product, even if they're not logging in every day. The one thing it doesn't mean is sticking your most valuable content behind filters buried 14 clicks deep in a product rarely visited. That's not magic at all.

To recap, before you start designing or coding anything it's worth asking yourself some of the following questions:

◊   Is this a real problem people want solved?
◊   Do I have experience with this problem that will help solve it?
◊   Can I build something that's magical, and is substantially better than existing products?

Answering affirmatively to the above questions means you've got the foundation of what it takes to build good software. Of course, the kicker is that it's not enough to just have a great idea. It requires great execution too. That's what we'll explore next.

How will you build it?

Foreword by Paul Adams, VP of Product

————

When I joined Intercom there was no one whose job title said Product Manager or Product Designer. It was myself, Darragh (leading the engineering team), 6-8 engineers and our founders. For the first six months, the team was a nebulous bubble with huge overlap in responsibilities. I was the product designer, I was the product manager and I was the researcher, but so was everyone else to some degree.

Our process for building product was very fluid. We recorded our entire product roadmap on a whiteboard. We kept things very simple, a list of projects we wanted to build, each of which was focused on one very clear problem to solve, and how long we thought it was going to take. Every project was less than four weeks long. We were obsessed with shipping, and wanted to get product into the hands of our customers as soon as we could so we could learn if we had solved the problem for them.

We outgrew this process when we hit about 20 people in our product and engineering team, but we still retain the core principles from the early days about how we build product:

◊ **We have a ruthless focus on the exact problem we're trying to solve**. We do this by obsessively talking to customers and researching their problems, perceptions, wants and needs. Our PMs are directly connected to customers.

When I think back to the companies I worked at earlier in my career, people were not obsessed with the specifics of the problems the same way we are at Intercom. Many product ideas people had were not real world problems. Often they were the ideas of a senior person, pulled from an anecdote from their life. In rare cases these ideas worked, but in most cases they failed. At Intercom we don't work that way. We need to know we're spending our precious resources on real problems that lots of our customers have. We don't have the luxury of guessing.

◊ **We obsess about the smallest thing we can build that we think will solve the problem**. We think big, but we scope right back to the absolute minimum. We are ruthless with scope. This is a painful process, but this pain means you're remaining focused.

◊ **We ship to learn**. Shipping is only the beginning of building product. We ship as fast and frequently as we can. A lot of startups misinterpret this idea as throwing shit at the wall and seeing what sticks. We're not fans of lots of multivariate testing. We don't run experiments. Startups that fall back to experiments to make product decisions aren't focusing enough on the problem they're solving.

Shipping to learn is more about being confident that you've understood and solved the problem, but humble enough to know you'll only truly learn when it's in the hands of customers. All the best product people I've worked with are obsessively curious after they ship something. They *need* to know if what they designed and built helped their customers.

This combination has in many ways been our secret. We obsess over the problem to be solved, we stay laser focused on the problem, we ruthlessly scope solutions that we believe will solve this very focused problem and we ship knowing that we have a lot to learn.

Many people have written about how internet businesses *should* build software, but there are few examples where startups show *how* it happens. Quite often it's a messy reality few want to share.

Since we started Intercom we've learned a lot about scaling a product building team, and the nitty gritty involved in getting valuable product out the door as fast as possible.

Things to keep in mind:

◊ This process reflects how we built product in an earlier iteration of Intercom when our team was about four product managers, four product designers and 25 product engineers. The team has grown substantially since then, so it's not the exact process we use today.

◊ How we build product is heavily influenced by our culture. Your culture is different, so what you do should be different. Nonetheless there are some general principles that we've used to great effect, which will help you think about how you build your product.

1. CREATE A SET OF GUIDELINES FOR MAKING DECISIONS

In order to grow and scale a product team, you need a set of values to help you make good decisions that align with what you collectively believe. That's why we have a set of guidelines.

Many small steps are better than bigger launches

Greatness is achieved in 1,000 small steps. Ship the smallest, simplest thing that will get you closest to your objective as fast as possible and help you learn what works.

Think about daily and weekly goals

Every single day of work counts. Every individual should know what their goals are for each day, how they relate to the team's weekly goal and how they relate to what is being released by the company.

Optimize for face-to-face collaboration

Work moves faster face-to-face. Two people at a whiteboard generate more ideas and reach consensus quicker than any other setup we've seen. Remote work can be great for many things, but not for speed and efficiency of decision making.

Fight against "work work"

Using software to build software is often slower than using whiteboards and sticky notes. Fight anything beyond a lightweight process and use the fewest number of software tools to get the job done.

The outcome matters much more than the plan

Plans are made with the information available at the time but things only become fully clear as you execute. The best teams absorb and react to new information and are able to build great product in spite of changing circumstances.

"The MVP philosophy gets misused. It doesn't mean ship crap product fast. Don't focus on the minimum and forget about the viable. Test a prototype with your target users before you ship and you'll ensure the first thing you ship is an MVP or better."

– SIAN (DIRECTING PRODUCT RESEARCH)

---

2. DEMAND CLEAR ACCOUNTABILITY

When building product, it must be *crystal clear* who is accountable for what. If it's a design problem, it's on the designer (next time around ensure they understand the research and the problem you're addressing). If the product is shipped with too many bugs, it's on the PM (next time ensure they test realistic usage and edge cases).

Product building teams have natural grey areas and collaboration often means a better end result. So people within teams work this out themselves. But when it comes to analyzing what your team spends their precious time building, the lines of accountability need to be very clear.

3. CREATE A LIGHTWEIGHT, TRANSPARENT ROADMAP

A good roadmap draws from a few primary sources (more on this shortly). Ours is based on things we believe in, new ideas we have, features that help us scale, qualitative feedback from customers and quantitative data based on measuring performance of our product.

The challenge is balancing these ingredients and synthesizing them into a clear plan for what to build over the next few months.

When Intercom had a relatively small product team a really effective way to do that was to think about our product roadmap over three timelines: the next six years, six months and six weeks.

The next six years
This should be your picture of the world six years from now, taking into account how it will have evolved because of the change you enacted.

The next six months
This is your plan for building things that will make a significant impact on your journey toward the change you want to enact in the world. When you look at what you will build over the next six months you should be thinking, "We're making great progress."

Your six month plan is subject to change. Looking ahead six months, about 50-75% of things on the list might be built, while the other 25% might be things you hadn't thought of before. This is a rolling timeline that is updated every couple of months.

AS THE LENGTH OF YOUR CYCLE GROWS, YOUR CONFIDENCE IN DELIVERING ON IT DROPS DRAMATICALLY

1 week

6 week

3 month

6 month

Accuracy

Length of plan

The next six weeks

The plan for the next six weeks is very concrete. This is your immediate plan and what your team intimately understands. You know exactly what's being built. Design work is well underway. This is a rolling timeline that is updated every week or two.

4. CREATE A CULTURE OF GOAL SETTING

To ensure you stay focused and on track, set weekly goals for your team. Daily and weekly goals are a great way of helping you prioritize. The volume of stuff that comes up daily for a product team, added to the gravitational pull of seemingly meaningful distractions, makes it essential to have weekly goals.

To hit weekly goals, break them out as daily and sub-daily goals. This reinforces the idea that every day counts and reaffirms that the cadence of building matters.

Our process for building product is by no means perfect. We iterate on it constantly, and by the time you read this, we will have tweaked it again. Nonetheless, these four principles are a great starting point to reflect on how you build product and ultimately help you improve.

THE ANATOMY OF A PRODUCT ROADMAP

Deciding what goes on your roadmap requires tough decisions and agonizing trade-offs. Should you build exciting new products or iterate on your existing product? Should you build features needed by prospective customers or focus on building around existing customer problems?

We've worked really hard to ensure we have a balanced set of priorities. To aid this, we bucket all the ideas we have into five categories:

1. New ideas we have
These are based on opinion rather than research. They include trends we see and ideas we have. They're not data driven. They come from looking around us and seeing what excites us most.

For example, we knew we wanted emoji and stickers throughout Intercom. We knew it was an important part of modern messaging. Customers weren't asking for them. But we built them because we believed in them and people love them.

2. Iterate recently shipped products
A common mistake most software companies make is shipping something and moving on to the next shiny thing. But one of the truths of building software is that you never fully get it right the first time. This is universally true, no matter how hard you try and no matter how much research you do. So we commit to making sure shipping is just the beginning and then we iterate and make things better. This takes deliberate planning and perseverance.

This is made much easier by knowing your success criteria prior to shipping. So we set success criteria, often in the form of metrics, measure them post launch and then follow up with customers where necessary for qualitative feedback.

3. Our most common customer problems
Every week, our product management team reads hundreds of customer conversations. As our customer support team talks with customers, they diligently tag every conversation with a category (e.g. usability issue, feature request, bug) and they also tag the team that owns that area of the product.

Once a week, our PMs scan these conversations and reach out to customers directly to learn more. On top of this, every few months our research team takes all the conversations, analyzes them and creates a "hit list" of the most common customer problems. Using the PMs' weekly pulse and the researchers' systematic analyses, we can easily determine which problems to address first.

4. Improving quality

All software has bugs. Aiming for zero bugs is unrealistic, impractical and certainly overly optimistic for something that gives you fast diminishing returns. So all issues need to be graded on a scale so you know which ones are most important. We use two primary measures for grading:

- ◊ How severe is the problem?
- ◊ How many customers does it affect?

You must fiercely commit to a high bar for speed, latency and efficiency in what you build. It's not glamorous, but much of what we ship simply addresses bugs.

5. Features to help you scale

Finally, if you're a fast growing company, you're likely seeing new problems with your product as your company grows. You're onboarding customers that are bigger than you've seen before. You're signing up customers from industries that you haven't seen before.

While you should never build a feature to close a deal – that signals the beginning of the end for your product – having conversations with your sales team is an excellent way to research new types of potential customers and to understand the types of features they're looking for.

FINDING THE RIGHT BALANCE

With these five inputs, the art is balancing competing demands. How can we build exciting new products, iterate on our existing product, deliver commonly requested features from existing customers and add new features needed by prospective customers, all while keeping everything high quality, bug free, fast and performant?

Enter the world of hard trade-offs. If you develop only items from the "new ideas" list you'll have an app that's half-useless, half-finished, buggy and slow. Likewise if you just address the "most common customer problems" you'll solve the problems customers have today, but ignore the ones they might have tomorrow.

SHIPPING IS ONLY THE BEGINNING

All too often, shipping product is seen as an end, a milestone reached, a good time to move onto the next project, an even better time to move onto another team. In fact, the opposite is true. Shipping is the beginning.

> **"Software only becomes valuable when you ship it to customers. Before then it's just a costly accumulation of hard work and assumptions."**
> – DARRAGH (GROWING ENGINEERING FROM 1 TO 90 PEOPLE)

To encourage this mindset in our team, we follow three principles:

1. Be comfortable knowing new features aren't perfect
You can't become good at something without the freedom to be bad at it first. If you believe every idea you present must look and sound great, don't be surprised if you have very few of them. If you have very few don't be surprised if you pick a bad one. When you pick a bad idea no amount of iteration will make it great.

We've often shipped things that weren't "perfect". There is always a list of things that could be better, and additional features that could be added. But we deliberately chose not to build them in order to accelerate production. We believe that shipping is a company's heartbeat and that we quickly learn from our customers whether what we left out is more important than we thought.

2. Carefully define self-contained, well-scoped projects
Self-contained projects mean that engineers don't have to understand lots of different parts of the codebase to get building. This is great for new people because they can jump right in. Well-scoped projects mean being able to ship something within a week.

The temptation is always to bite off something bigger, something more ambitious, something more groundbreaking. But the opposite approach often works better: paint the bigger picture, then break it down into lots of smaller pieces that ship bit by bit, gradually replacing parts of the experience. This means being comfortable knowing that parts of the product are inconsistent, but it also means you can adapt and learn as you continuously push code to production.

3. Shipping is about learning

You can never fully predict how users will behave or react. You need to give people a basic feature set, see how they behave, and iterate quickly from there. We ship to learn. We know that we will be wrong more often than we will be right. Because we care most about learning, we prioritize speed to execution.

> "The quicker you can get feedback on what you're thinking, the better your idea will be. Usage is oxygen for ideas."
>
> – DES (CO-FOUNDER)

We all get excited dreaming about all the amazing things our product will do. As a designer you envision one cohesive beautiful thing. As a developer you map it out: every method, class and edge case. A small piece of value you could have shipped months ago, that your customers would have loved, can teach you so much more.

What will you charge?

Foreword by Des Traynor, Co-Founder and Chief Strategy Officer

———

We didn't charge a single cent during Intercom's first year. All we did was work on product. At the end of that year we were ready to think about the value we were delivering and how to charge for it.

Initially we spent weeks dreaming up fancy pricing models, running the numbers, analyzing our customer base to see who gets most value and deciding what should be free. During that time we met with Jason Fried, Co-Founder of Basecamp, and his advice was characteristically simple, "Just charge $50 and see what happens". *Are you serious?*

He was.

Charging $50/month was a smart move because it brought customers past the "why not" threshold. It's a *considered* purchase. I worry about business products that charge just $9/month; it can give them a false sense of traction. Their conversion and churn will look good, but only because no one in any credible company even notices $9/month on a company credit card. If the plan is to move that $9 to $59 when things "get real", then I'd argue the business is still none the wiser about whether or not customers will pay it.

So $50 was a good divider. It taught us a lot about our user base. It helped us distinguish credible customers from folks who were just playing around.

We changed our pricing structure a year later to something that distinguished the different types of customers and types of value served. If you look at any successful business they will always iterate on their pricing as they learn more about their business and their customers.

People often dispute why companies change their prices but the logic is very simple. You don't have as much information about your business before you start charging as you do afterward. So you might realize you need to drop your pricing, tweak it, or charge bigger companies more or smaller ones less. Secondly if you continue to improve your product then it will inherently deliver more value to more people and cost you more to support and scale, so naturally you may need to change prices to account for that.

But when you're starting up, your goal for pricing should be to get some meaningful cash from people to learn what pricing works and what doesn't. Metrics like user engagement are definitely relevant in the early days, but if your plan is to sell valuable software to businesses then you shouldn't wait too long to test if it's really valuable.

At every startup, no matter what stage you're at, you should ask yourself: What can we charge for our product? It can seem like an insurmountable task to get right, especially if you've never priced anything before, but it's something you should come to grips with as soon as possible rather than putting it off until the future.

Here's the thing, there's no easy answer or solution, just you, your business and the ultimate need to make money from what you're doing. But you should start charging your customers as early as you can, because it helps you discover the most important areas to focus on.

As you're doing that, you'll quickly find that every startup faces four common pricing pitfalls, creating a vicious cycle which usually results in putting off charging *anything* indefinitely.

1. Believing *everyone* should be happy to pay for your product
2. Believing there is some mythical "perfect" price which extracts maximum revenue from every single customer
3. Believing product pricing can never be changed once established
4. Delaying charging indefinitely as a result of 1, 2 and 3

Pricing your product can sometimes feel like pulling a number out of thin air, and to a point it is. As Jason Fried says, "Put a price on it, and see what happens."

One thing to remember is that the longer you wait to charge for your product, the more normalized the "free" part is and the scarier it gets to ask for money.

Regardless of whether you're selling a SaaS service or a physical good, you need to understand what it takes to attract your target customer and then decide what you want to charge them. That gives you the ability to plot *how* you'll reach those customers, which gives you three options: transactional, enterprise and self-service.

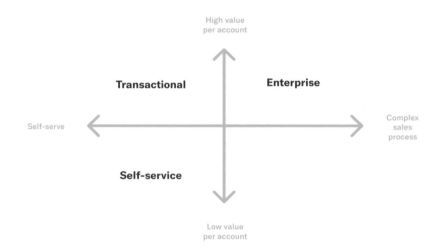

These axes were created by Chaotic Flow's Joel York to define the three key sales models for SaaS businesses and are a great way to help you understand how to move forward. The bottom right quadrant, a complex sales process with low value customers, doesn't produce a viable business so it's not even worth considering.

Whether your business is an app or a restaurant, you need to first understand what it takes to attract your target customer and decide how much revenue you want to earn from them.

The problem is that many startups, when using this model to define themselves, end up in the bottom left quadrant as it's the easiest one to scale in.

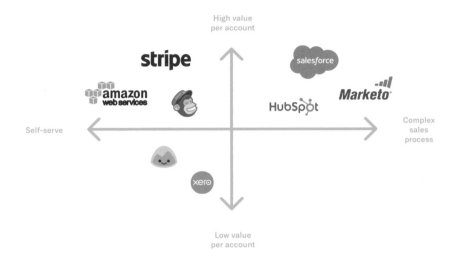

Being in the lower left quadrant means you usually end up with a high amount of low value customers. This limits how you can acquire customers. The economics of spending $300 to acquire customers for a $99 product are all wrong.

So depending on which industry you're in, picking the wrong quadrant could leave you dead before you even start building anything at all. Here are some examples:

◊ Some industries are notoriously hard to reach, e.g. content marketing isn't as effective for dentists as it is for developers. This means you might need to pay to acquire customers.
◊ Some industries deal in annual contracts, NDAs and SLAs. This means you need to invest in a sales process.
◊ Some industries are used to PowerPoint sales presentations, handheld onboarding and onsite training. This means you need a high contract value to profit on a customer.

Evaluating if you're able to offer a self-serve experience or complex sales process and then determining if there's a high or low value for each user helps you decide how you should approach the customer.

If your customers are high value with a complex sales process, you'll likely need a sales team to do the work. Whereas if your users are low value and able to serve themselves, you should invest more heavily in marketing to do the work for you.

Some companies, like GitHub, live in a special place across two quadrants.

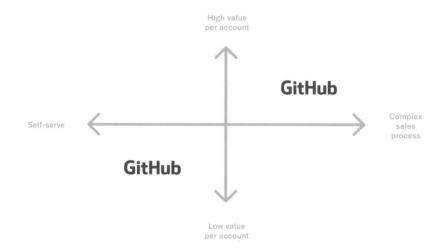

GitHub competes at the $7 per month price point for end users, but also sells GitHub Enterprise for $21 per user per month to large companies. On that end of the scale, the company has sales and account managers to service that quadrant specifically.

> "Low pricing rules out lots of potential customers for your product, in the same way serving $3 steaks in a restaurant actually restricts your clientele."
>
> – DES (CO-FOUNDER)

PRICING FOR VALUE

The key to selling your product is understanding the value it delivers to your customers and then positioning it correctly based on that. A great example of this is how the toothpaste industry struggled to convince people of toothpaste's value when selling it as "prevention from gum disease" as opposed to "beautiful teeth."

The same is true in the software industry. $29 a month sounds expensive for "5GB of file storage" but great value for "the certainty of keeping your family photos safe forever." It's about understanding why your customers buy your product, and then positioning it properly.

The problem in SaaS is that there are traditionally three tiers of pricing: small, medium and large. Each tier gives customers more accounts, emails sent or API calls, etc. Imposing this type of "step function" pricing implies that your customers are going to fall into three neat buckets. In reality the value each customer gets falls across a spectrum.

Some customers might log in once a month, while others spend eight hours a day, five days a week living in your product. If you only have small, medium and large plans, you are creating a difference between the value they get and how much they pay you because each plan has an upper threshold for cost.

Ironically, unlimited plans are the worst for you because they're essentially designed to give the largest customers, often with the most means to pay, the largest discount.

Often behind the scenes, these pricing plans are designed around the incremental cost to your company. Instead, your plans should focus on the clear value offered to the user which is the difference they'll actually be paying for.

If you can find a pain point that resonates with your audience, you might not even need to change a single line of code to start selling or upselling your product to people.

Understanding that there's more cost to using your product than just money is important. When you ask your users to do something it needs to be framed in a way that fulfills their needs and desires.

Your customers aren't just investing money into your product, but also time, data and effort to learn something new, and it's easy to forget that.

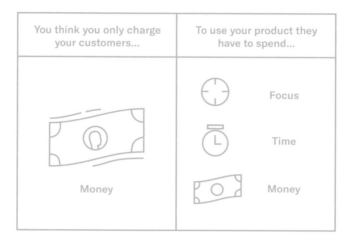

You think you only charge your customers...	To use your product they have to spend...
Money	Focus Time Money

 Key idea

Cash isn't the only thing businesses spend. When customers say your product is too expensive they're not necessarily talking about your price.

FOUR PRICING PRINCIPLES FOR YOUR PRODUCT

Armed with this knowledge, how should you guide your pricing discussions? These four pricing principles can help you determine where your focus should lie.

1. Charge earlier than you're comfortable with

Charging early delivers the right kind of customer feedback. Customers who don't pay for software give different feedback from those that do, and are the wrong people to take feedback from. As a rule of thumb, feedback from non-paying users tends to focus on additions to the product. Feedback from paying customers focuses on improvements to the product you already have.

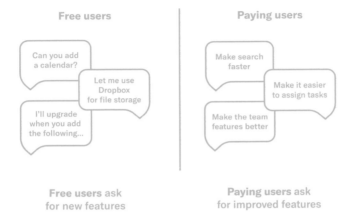

Free users

> Can you add a calendar?

> Let me use Dropbox for file storage

> I'll upgrade when you add the following...

Paying users

> Make search faster

> Make it easier to assign tasks

> Make the team features better

Free users ask for new features

Paying users ask for improved features

At Trello, the team struggled to put a price on their product and finally said, "It doesn't matter. We just need to pick something. So we should charge this flat rate because people will pay for it." It turned out that people did, but that presented a problem later. It was hard to move away from that flat rate, and a lot of money was left on the table.

> "It shouldn't be a surprise when you start getting your first paying customers. You should be confident you're delivering a product people are happy to pay for."
>
> – DES (CO-FOUNDER)

Michael Pryor, CEO at Trello, said that while it was a good solution at the time, the company took too long before revisiting it and could've been charging customers a lot more each month since users fell across a spectrum of usage habits.

The upside to flat rate plans is you'll quickly drop people who would never pay. The negative is that companies with extremely heavy usage habits pay the same amount as those that barely use your tool, and you'll be missing out on that money.

2. Charge more than you're comfortable with
It's easy to fall into the trap of charging a "small" monthly fee for your product, such as $19, to attract small-to-medium sized businesses. Even a four person company probably has $16K in monthly outgoings, which puts that price in perspective.

If you're charging less than the cost of your customer's office morning coffee run, and your tool is providing invaluable benefits for them, you're doing something wrong.

One mistake many startups make is offering a "top-tier" unlimited plan, which offers your largest customers significant discounts. Josh Pigford, Founder of Baremetrics, found that offering an unlimited plan "puts a hard cap on your revenue while giving away the farm." The types of customers who use your unlimited plans are the ones who are happy to pay far more than you're already charging, and probably get the most value from you as well.

Don't be afraid to charge people for what they're really using and, as mentioned earlier, sell them on the value you'll be delivering.

3. Justify (or kill) your lowest price point

A lot of services include a "starter" plan for \$5 or \$9 per month. Usually that's to reinforce the claim that the product is "affordable enough for everyone", while boosting your numbers.

Many of your costs are spread across all your customers, but some, such as Cost Per Acquisition and Cost To Serve are fixed regardless of the pricing plan. A customer on the \$9 plan costs just as much to acquire and can cost as much to support as your customers on the top-tier \$49 plan.

Worse yet, those tiny customers very rarely grow into higher priced tiers. Small companies can grow into large customers, but more often they remain a small customer paying the same amount forever. Many companies have chosen to kill their lowest priced plan after realizing this, lowering their support costs and increasing their revenue.

4. Plan to change your prices

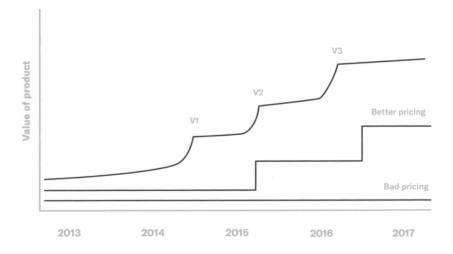

A common mistake is to never change your pricing. As you improve your product by adding features, speeding it up or in other ways, it's worth regularly reviewing your pricing and asking yourself some questions:

◊   Are we delivering more value than we were two years ago?
◊   Are our new customers less price-sensitive than previous ones?
◊   Has our marketing improved?

If you can answer yes to any one of these, it's time to review your pricing. When you do, document the ways your product has been updated and use that to justify it to your customers.

The fear of changing pricing is often a fear of customer complaints. "Grandfathering" mitigates a lot of this, as current customers are moved onto the new plan at their old pricing and new customers won't know the difference.

THERE'S NO SILVER BULLET FOR PRICING

Of all of the things you can spend time tweaking, pricing will yield the best return. One study by McKinsey & Company found that a one percent increase in pricing affects profits more than any other change. For some reason, never updating your product seems ludicrous, yet never updating your *pricing* doesn't?

As with all matters of pricing, there's no one way to do it, but there are lots of wrong turns and dead ends. Learn from them, adjust and decide if you're being sufficiently rewarded for the value you're delivering.

Who should you hire?

Foreword by Eoghan McCabe, Co-Founder and CEO

———

The first hire we made was Ben McRedmond, who now runs our Growth team. He was an engineer we'd known for a long time, so it made perfect sense. We were a software company so we hired engineers. If we were a plumbing company, we would have hired a plumber.

But he was also a generalist, exactly the type of person we needed at that stage. The fewer people you have, the more general each person's role ends up being; everyone has to wear many hats. As the company grows, you hire a lot of different specialists. But in the early days, generalists are best because you need people who are ready to pitch in wherever needed.

Ben was also unique because he was at the very start of his career. I truly believe in matching growing companies with growing people. Building a company requires learning about the world, figuring out who you are and improving. It's the same process you follow as an individual. If you can match a company that wants to grow with a set of people that want to grow, and their interests and ideals are aligned, your company will be set for success.

Finding your first few hires is incredibly difficult. You're no good at hiring yet. You don't have a clear idea of what your company is, so you don't know what you need. This means you're going to hire the wrong people. There's almost certainly going to be mismatches from the get-go. So early on it's important to have open, honest conversations among your founders about what a great candidate looks like for your company.

When all of Intercom could fit on one Hangout

It should go without saying, but you really have to like your first few hires. In the best situation, they will become your lifelong friends. You'll grow up together, get old together and share in success and failure together. That doesn't necessarily mean you should hire your friends, but hire people who share your fundamental values, who you feel very comfortable with and enjoy the company of.

In the early days, you've got to work very hard, in close quarters and in some incredibly stressful situations. Everyone is going to be some degree of pretty shit at what they do. It helps if the people involved want to be in the trenches with each other. I know Intercom wouldn't have worked if the founders hadn't liked each other.

Most people think the way a startup works is that you have a smart idea and then you hire a team to implement it. But that's actually much harder than it sounds. There are many reasons your startup might fail, but one of the biggest dangers is hiring the wrong people.

TOP 10 REASONS STARTUPS FAIL

Based on an analysis of 101 startup post-mortems

No market need	42%
Ran out of cash	29%
Not the right team	**23%**
Get outcompeted	19%
Pricing/cost issues	18%
Poor marketing	17%
Ignore customers	17%
Product mistimed	14%
Lose focus	14%
Disharmony on team/investors	13%

Credit: CB Insights

When you're such a small team, each hire has a disproportionately large impact. If your startup is still at an early stage, a bad hire has the potential to set you back several quarters and possibly even ruin the whole company. Faced with such high stakes, it's no surprise some people struggle to make a decision about who to hire.

One of the best ways to make sure your first hires are successful is to build a great founding team. Great people have a magnetic quality and attract other great people who want to work with them. Of course, you can offer them a huge salary, motivate people around an ambitious mission and give them interesting problems to solve. But in the software industry, there are many companies offering these things.

On the other hand, the people that you hire are proprietary. They're the one thing your competitors can't copy. So by hiring great people, you will motivate even more people to join, and the people who've already joined will know you're serious about making your company successful.

The type of people you hire will depend on your own unique culture and the needs of your business. But no matter what, making your team great requires that you recruit some truly special individuals. Here are some of the traits that we think separate the great from the good.

> "It's very easy to let yourself panic when hiring. You need to take a step back and think about the long-term impact of hiring the wrong person. Hiring desperately for your immediate circumstances can cause long-term damage."
> – MAGGIE (INTERCOM RECRUITING LEADER)

WHO SHOULD YOU HIRE? EXCEPTIONAL PEOPLE

A company's hiring process is usually a pretty good indicator of the quality of people at the company. The higher the bar, the better the talent, the more interesting the company.

Our VP of Engineering, Darragh, has been instrumental in teaching us what a good engineer looks like. He knew the difference between good and not-good-enough and has an innate sense of what makes an exceptional hire – the people who everyone fights to work with. As it turns out, these traits are just as applicable for non-engineers.

Exceptional people...are ambitious, and determined
◊ They dream big and push themselves, you and your team, towards bigger achievements than you initially thought possible.
◊ They have a growth mindset. They crave feedback and new challenges that will push them to grow. They persist in the face of setbacks, they see effort as the path to mastery, and they're inspired by and learn from the success of others.

Why this matters
Ambition is a ceiling to success. Great companies have huge ambition, which initially comes from the founders, but is sustained and thrives with the addition of ambitious people they hire. Ambitious and determined people fight for impact and push for greatness. They outperform and grow faster than people who may be more talented but lack an inner drive. Bet on them, and spend your time helping ambitious people grow.

Exceptional people...habitually simplify
They don't assume anything and strip big ideas back to their first principles. They know that greatness is achieved in 1,000 small steps. They also have a long term vision of where the technology they own should evolve to.

Why this matters
The default path for growing and evolving software is that it becomes more complex over time. Every single change will probably make your system more complex, unless the people you hire are deliberate about simplifying.

Exceptional people...help others be great
◊ Great people are those that everyone wants to work with.
◊ They understand that they can have more impact by helping those around them to learn, improve and thrive.
◊ They take care of the unglamorous or mundane quickly, effectively and without fuss.
◊ They aren't selfish with the hard problems. They know that others need challenges to grow and they support them well, but at the same time they regularly demonstrate their ability to solve hard problems efficiently.

◊ They're good teachers. They're patient and they adapt to support the different learning styles of those around them.

Why this matters

Companies that don't grow, die. Companies that grow, thrive. The same is true of people and teams. Hire people that fight for growth in those around them.

Exceptional people...know what's valuable

◊ They're customer focused, not just technology focused.

◊ They're ambitious and make sure they're solving big valuable problems.

◊ They weed out inefficiencies in process and communication and act like they're spending their own money.

Why this matters

A company can only scale if teams are trusted and empowered to be autonomous over their area of ownership and objectives. At any point, there are multiple ideas to explore and things to fix or iterate on, but you've only got a small bucket of time and resources. Trust comes when you know your people will fill that bucket with the right things.

Exceptional people...are creative and positive

◊ When things are difficult they give everyone hope and courage.

◊ They encourage possibilities. Instead of saying "that will never work", they understand the problem and what's valuable, and give those around them options.

◊ They are leaders who try to solve complex problems, not victims who blame others when they can't.

◊ They push for and encourage innovation both in the product they're building and in how they're building it.

◊ Their positivity is balanced with healthy skepticism. They're more focused on whether what they create works properly, than celebrating victory once it appears to work.

Why this matters

The default path for startups is toward failure. A team that thinks it's going to lose, will lose. Positivity is infectious and brings out the best in people. A team that has belief that they will succeed and is constantly creative in its efforts to succeed has a chance.

HOW TO HIRE EXCEPTIONAL PEOPLE

How do you know someone will have an exceptional impact after you hire them? The simple answer is that you don't. But you can look for signs during the interview process that will help you make an educated guess.

> "In the early days, it's impossible for you to understand how much of a game changer it can be to hire truly brilliant people. It creates a momentum that attracts even more brilliant people. Great people beget great people."
>
> – EOGHAN (CO-FOUNDER)

"Culture fit"

Many companies try to interview for "culture fit" and the term has earned a justifiably poor reputation. Without proper training and careful execution this can easily become, "How similar is this person to me?"

Solely hiring people similar to your current team limits your company's capability and causes you to miss out on diverse ideas. You have cultural blindspots nobody is aware of. You may find yourself biased in unexpected ways: "This candidate probably wouldn't enjoy working with a younger team anyway," or "This job is too demanding for someone like this," or "We move too fast to sugarcoat feedback and I don't think they're emotionally strong enough to work with us."

Hearing anything like this from your team is a clear, unambiguous signal that your process is broken. Your culture may not be very healthy either. Facebook's excellent *Managing Unconscious Bias* series of videos should be a required part of training for your team, and not just for those involved in hiring.

Culture contribution

A lot of interviews – technical screeners, design mockups – are designed to be binary in their outcome. But determining how a candidate will improve your culture or identifying when they won't is incredibly difficult, with results necessarily spread across a spectrum.

In the early days, you're looking for people who can cope with uncomfortable situations. You're moving fast in unexplored territory, so there will be upsets, setbacks and mistakes. The right people respond positively in these situations. They identify the problem and correct it, learning from the mistake and ensuring nobody else has to learn it the hard way.

BE CLEAR ABOUT YOUR VALUES

It's essential to tell every candidate the values that are important to your company. This isn't a quiz show. Candidates shouldn't have to guess what matters to you. It's a poor interview if you're left wondering: "Did they misunderstand my question or just answer poorly?" Explaining your values gives a candidate more information about your culture too. It should be a completely acceptable outcome for them to say: "You value that? I'm out of here!".

A good approach is to ask for precise examples from their experience to help you understand how they'll behave if they join your company. Details are important.

For example, one of Intercom's strongest values is, "Every day counts". Our competitors are constantly improving. The market continues to expect more. We hire smart people and remove obstacles in their path, so we won't hire people who introduce their own obstacles e.g "I knew the code was broken but it wasn't my job to fix it." If they didn't jump in and fix it, did they tell someone it was broken? Did they suggest a way to fix it? What did they do to make sure it didn't break again?

SHOULD YOU GO WIDE OR GO DEEP?

When your company is comprised of a handful of people in one room, everyone has to do everything by necessity. This means the first few hires you make have to run the full gamut, from product strategy, to bug fixes, to marketing and more.

A lot of startups might refer to this person as a "unicorn". This is a misnomer. Unicorns don't actually exist; generalists do. It is entirely reasonable to expect smart people to possess the knowledge and skills needed to think holistically across all levels of a product. In your early days, having these naturally curious and passionate people who soak up everything around them is essential.

In fact, curiosity is the single most important attribute for an early stage team. Without it, you're limited by the existing skills new hires bring with them. No matter how proficient an engineer, designer or product manager, they'll need to learn different skills on demand.

People who possess an insatiable curiosity will learn and adapt while pushing your team forward in ways you could never predict. When something new is required of them, they immediately research the subject, not because it's their job, but because they're so invested in the company's success.

These generalists are the glue that holds your startup together. They know enough about a broad range of disciplines, can import ideas and influences from a variety of sources and can collaborate with everyone on their team.

AS YOU GROW, START THINKING ABOUT SPECIALISTS

For most companies, you eventually reach the point where having someone who knows enough really isn't enough. As teams scale, it becomes necessary to add people who are true masters of their craft. These people devote themselves to expertise in their chosen area. They are the engineers who live and breathe infrastructure and availability and the visual designers who are obsessed with grids and color theory.

Specialists magnify advantages. They bring a degree of experience and domain knowledge that a generalist never could. They dig deep into the entire range of local solutions. They apply a level of polish and professionalism to their niche of the product that their generalist colleagues could never achieve. They coach and advise others in their area of expertise. It's like adding rocket fuel to your team; they make all output along one specific dimension immeasurably better.

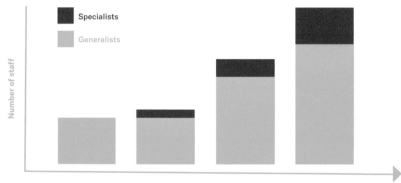

So who you hire depends the stage your company is at. At an early stage startup, you should hire generalists. As your team matures and you encounter the murkier corners of your domain, start bringing in specialists. At Intercom we currently aim for a ratio of 5:1 for generalists to specialists. That means we have people with skills broad enough to ship quality product, but narrow enough to raise the bar in the places that really matter.

CHAPTER FIVE

Do culture and values matter?

Foreword by Eoghan McCabe, Co-Founder and CEO

————

Intercom was a little different from a lot of startups in that the founders had been working together for more than five years beforehand. So our values were already aligned. We remained interested in working with each other over many years and many different companies because we fundamentally shared the same principles.

This meant that our culture evolved in a very organic fashion at the start. We didn't need to codify our values – the founders had that shared context, having worked side by side for so long on a daily basis. In fact, if you try to force it early on I think you lose an opportunity to allow the nuances of your values to flourish and take shape. Codifying values really early on means you're faking it; you don't really know yet what values work and what don't. The most meaningful values and the most meaningful cultures emerge in an organic fashion.

Later on, when you're doing things at scale and you're hiring people who go on to hire people in quick succession themselves, you need to provide tools and frameworks to help them do so successfully. That's when you start to codify things.

Pretty early on, we came up with five or six values that were heavily oriented around things the company cared about at that point in time: making good product and doing so in a timely fashion. One of our earliest values is one we still have to this day: "Think big, start small". It's always helped people focus on how they spend their time every day, and reminds us to limit the size of everything we build rather than overcomplicate things.

Our values have always been a little looser than at other companies. We were lucky enough to be a founding team of four who were already philosophically aligned. Most founding teams are typically two people, and in many cases you spend years getting on the same page. You might have to hire people who you don't know, and then you're going to have to spend even more time getting them on the same page.

If you want your company to be driven by values, and you're not as fortunate as we were to have strong relationships and principles in place from day zero, someone's going to have to take the initiative early on to force those values on the group. This will create some unavoidable friction and tension, but it's an important opportunity for shared growth and development.

When most people think about company culture, they think about something contained within four walls in a specific place. They might think about ping pong tables and a fridge full of soda.

A company culture is none of these things. It's actually people practicing the spoken and unspoken values of the company on a consistent and deliberate basis.

Subsequently, it means you can't buy – or fake – culture. It's relatively straightforward to create the illusion of a happy, open and inclusive workplace. Unless you have a real culture, the illusion will quickly fade, regardless of how hard you try to engineer it. Jason Fried, co-founder of Basecamp, once said, "Real cultures are built over time. They're the result of action, reaction, and truth."

You can't force culture, but you can give it the chance to flourish. At Zappos, managers are tasked with one goal – maintaining company culture. Instead of tying them up in meetings and bureaucracy, managers empower people to make the right decisions for the company and customer. They do this through five weeks of training on company culture, taking calls from customers and working in the Zappos warehouse. It's only then that they start the job they were hired for.

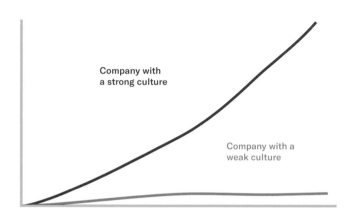

Company with
a strong culture

Company with a
weak culture

Your startup might not have the resources of Zappos, but there are similar
steps you can take to make sure culture flourishes. You could put out a
culture book written by employees about what your company culture
means to them. Or you could have everyone spend one day a month doing
customer support. We do this at Intercom – we refer to them as "Customer
Days" – and it helps everyone stay in touch with Intercom's mission, as
well as with the people who pay for and use our products.

HAPPINESS AT WORK IS ABOUT YOUR MISSION, NOT YOUR PERKS

A related but often overlooked consideration is happiness. Is your team
happy at work? Does that even matter if the job is getting done? As it
turns out, yes, it does matter deeply. But simply offering a bunch of
office perks isn't the answer. Free food, massages or on-site gyms
doesn't guarantee happiness or a healthy culture. The equation isn't
quite that simple; it's not perks in, happiness out.

Google, for example, has led the way in offering generous perks for a long time. But if that was the real answer to happiness at work, Google wouldn't stress so heavily that it's passion, not perks that is the biggest contributor to its success.

Tony Hsieh, CEO of Zappos, quite literally wrote the book on happiness at work and why it matters. In *Delivering Happiness*, he writes about how Zappos built culture intentionally by valuing happiness and nurturing employees. Small things, like offering new employees $2,000 if they quit after their first week, helps weed out bad company matches. But he also emphasizes that customer service is everyone's responsibility and promotes building strong teams outside the office.

"You can't have confidence in your values until you test them. Testing means pushing their boundaries. You're going to have to break them sometimes.
And that's okay."

– EOGHAN (CO-FOUNDER)

Your founding team and everyone who joins you along the way should regularly ask: "Why does our company exist other than to make money?" Most people can't actually answer that question succinctly, and that's a problem for culture and team building. Without a clear mission, it's easy to end up with feature bloat and a lack of cohesion within the product because everyone is working to their own end.

Twitter's mission statement was "To be the pulse of the planet" (it's changed a few times) while Amazon's is "To be earth's most customer-centric company; to build a place where people can come to find and discover anything they might want to buy online." Intercom's is "To make business personal".

A mission statement is the present-day expression of a strong, timeless vision, which, though it might sound abstract or grandiose, sets the stage for years to come. A company's vision should be robust and stand the test of time. Technologies, social networks and other trends come and go – your company should stay relevant regardless.

But a vision is more than that: it gives your employees something to rally around as a purpose, and tells everyone which direction they're going. That way, when there's conflict in a team, it's easier to decide whether the answer is no, or "Hell yeah". (A reference to Derek Sivers who said when deciding whether you should do something, if you feel anything less than "Absolutely! Hell yeah!" – then say "no.")

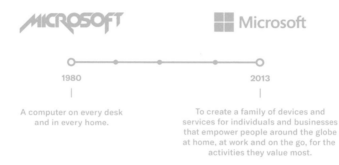

1980 — A computer on every desk and in every home.

2013 — To create a family of devices and services for individuals and businesses that empower people around the globe at home, at work and on the go, for the activities they value most.

So, what actions can you actually take to focus on company culture? Alexander Kjerulf, a Danish management consultant who styles himself as a "Chief Happiness Officer", offers five tips to foster a happy and healthy company culture:

◊ Practice random acts of workplace happiness
◊ Hire positive people
◊ Stop negative behavior
◊ Celebrate success
◊ Celebrate mistakes

Your culture will be based around the behavior you value most, but the above are a good starting point for any business.

MAINTAINING COMPANY CULTURE OVER TIME

As we discussed in the last chapter, when hiring at Intercom we intentionally question whether or not a person is a great addition to team culture. That doesn't mean you're looking for carbon copies of your founding team. Only hiring people similar to your current team won't improve how you work, and limits your entire company's capability. Every team has cultural blind spots they're unaware of, and you'll likely find yourself biased in unexpected ways.

What's important is that when you hire someone, they're *aligned* with your vision and mission. If someone's misaligned with these, the team they hire will be equally, if not more, misaligned. Before you know it, you've got multiple teams completely out of sync with your company's original culture.

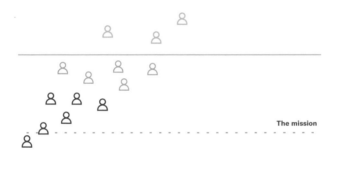

A great way to keep people aligned is to have people observe the work of their teammates on a regular basis. For example, every Friday at 5pm, everyone at Intercom gathers around the big screen in their office, people grab beers and colleagues demo what they worked on that week.

This reinforces many of the values we believe in – shipping fast, craving feedback and representing Intercom with pride.

Friday Show & Tell: An Intercom tradition since the early days of the company

Pixar have a similar approach. They host what they refer to as Pixar University, where employees devote four hours a week to learning new skills from their colleagues.

It's also important to remember that culture will become diluted as your team grows. When you walk down the hall and don't know whether someone's on your team, or just visiting, it's time to codify and lock in your values. By giving employees a place where they continually get to learn and evolve, everyone feels like they're part of a bigger whole. It also creates an environment where people are willing to collaborate, and genuinely like each other. Create a culture like that, and nobody will become misaligned.

How will you find your first customers?

Foreword by Des Traynor, Co-Founder and Chief Strategy Officer

————

In the very early days of Intercom, I used to literally email people and ask them to use Intercom. If you look at the first 200 emails I sent from my Intercom email, almost all of them were along the lines of, "Would you like to try Intercom?" For a customer who we really wanted, I'd mock up a screenshot showing how we'd nail a reasonable use case for their product. Anecdotally that helped people understand both what we could do for them and what it would look like in their product.

Emailing every customer certainly doesn't scale, but when you have zero customers, scaling is not the problem. Getting from zero to 100 is your challenge. And believe me, it's a grind. I spent day and night sending email after email in a cold, dark, horrid office in Dublin.

But it was incredibly rewarding in important ways. The replies flooded in and I quickly learned so much about the types of customers who were signing up. Our user onboarding was centered on one action: install a snippet of JavaScript into your product. But it turned out that not every business has a developer sitting idle waiting to tweak JavaScript. Not every business even has a developer. All of this reality hit home during those days and we learned so much about what it takes to help our customers get started.

Des Traynor
@destraynor

I'm up at 6am to run a webinar for good folks in Australia, New Zealand, India, Singapore and more. Starting now.

6:09 AM - Aug 2 2012

It wasn't just sending emails either. I remember getting up at 5 a.m. to give a webinar to nine people in the Southern Hemisphere. The webinar was a fusion of thought leadership mixed with product examples from Intercom. You question what the hell you're doing at the time, but out of that webinar we got nine customers. And those nine customers probably us got 90 and then 900. Wherever a customer was interested in using our product we'd show up. We've never afforded ourselves the luxury of being fussy.

These days things are quite different. When we launched our product Educate, it only took the team four weeks before they were celebrating hitting $1MM in ARR (Annual Recurring Revenue). The grumpy old man in me wants to tell them these stories so they realize that it doesn't always happen that quick.

In the good old days, starting a software business in any industry was really hard. Getting your foot in the door required not just a great idea but a massive upfront investment in building that product, never mind getting it in front of customers.

Today it's easier than ever to launch a software business. Everyone is building web and mobile apps. App stores have levelled the playing field and now anyone can publish an app on the same terms as a big company.

But when you ask most of these businesses what they're doing to actually acquire customers, you hear the usual suspects: cold emailing, social media marketing, SEO, content marketing, email marketing, the latest growth hacking miracle, etc. With few exceptions, it isn't working. Nobody is listening because there is so much noise.

That's because getting your first customers to actually pay for your product is one of the hardest things a startup will ever have to do. Succeeding validates your product's right to exist and shows that you might be on the right track after all.

HOW WE GOT OUR FIRST CUSTOMERS

It took us just over a year to get 100 people to pay for Intercom. This sounds like a long time, but when we launched, our product was free for everyone, and we actually didn't start charging for a year. Hence we always planned to wait a long time for customers to start paying us.

In terms of how we found them, we didn't; they found us. We planted many seeds in the lead up to our launch. For a long time, we'd been writing articles about how to run a SaaS business, how to scale a SaaS business, how to grow your audience, pick your features, delight your customers. It was the sort of content that would specifically appeal to folks working in SaaS companies. We'd built our own social proof. If you're sending cold emails and LinkedIn messages to people without that, don't be surprised when you get a nasty response.

Our content meant that when we launched our product with a blog post in 2011, we already had a captive audience and we got an immediate burst of signups.

Then the Intercom app was upvoted to #1 on Hacker News, which got us many more signups. We also wrote a very popular guest post for Smashing Magazine on topics related to Intercom, which expanded our audience even further. If you look at Intercom's first 100 paying customers, most came from one of these channels.

That's not to say "Traction = blog post + Hacker News + feature in TechCrunch." It's not that easy. And besides, it's Product Hunt these days. Any company can get a one-day bump on TechCrunch and then quickly find itself in the "trough of sorrow", as Uber's Andrew Chen calls it.

The Startup Curve

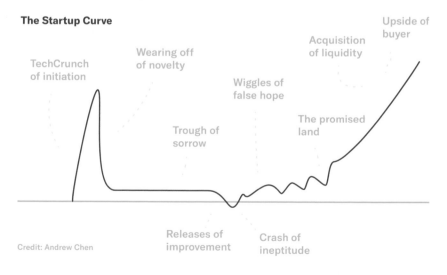

You need to find meaningful traction. And to do that in B2B SaaS, you need to push forward the ideas that are embodied in your software.

Let's say you are trying to pitch a new email app. New customers don't care much about the pixels, shadows or the typography of the product. Most of these products look the same: fancy sidebars and swipe actions. What customers really care about is the thinking behind the product: how you think about email and how those ideas are reflected in your product. If those ideas resonate with your audience they'll definitely give your product a try.

A great example of this is the famous internal memo, "We don't sell saddles here," that Slack CEO Stewart Butterfield published before the company launched. It clearly articulated the vision behind the product and how they thought about their competitors. As a result when the product was publicly available, people were queuing up to try it.

By all means, launch on Product Hunt, and if you do a good job there you'll get a few thousand people interested. But they're window shoppers, jumping from store to store. Easy come, easy go. To attract a meaningful audience of like-minded people you have to share the ideas at the core of your product as early as you can. That's what attracts the people who are interested in the ideas and purpose underpinning your product.

"All of our early customers were hand-held by the founders. This gave us a very explicit understanding of what we needed to build and helped not only bring in those customers but created a tight feedback loop where we were able to deliver improvements in the right way and on time."

– EOGHAN (CO-FOUNDER)

MAKING THE MOST OF WORD OF MOUTH

There are hundreds, if not thousands, of strategies for acquiring new customers, but word of mouth is probably *the* most powerful way of getting them. Put it this way, you're probably much more likely to try an app that a friend tells you about over coffee than one you see in a Google search ad.

Word of mouth is your first traffic source. It's hard to put a price on its value. And it's only useful when the same words come out of lots of different mouths.

You might have heard the story of the blind men and the elephant. It's a famous story about a group who argue over what they've encountered, because they are each only exposed to a small piece of it. Those at the tail think it's a rope, those at the trunk think it's a snake. In situations like this the elephant would struggle to get word of mouth. There's too many conflicting ideas about what it actually is.

This elephant, of course, is your product. As your product grows, the number of things it can and will be used for grows too. Let's say you have a time tracking app. Some people might say it's for tracking billable hours, while others will say it's for tracking vacations. Some will say it's a project management tool, while others call it a task list.

When people think very different things about your product, it's important to have great messaging. It helps people explain your product to other prospective customers.

Great messaging that encourages word of mouth is simple, compelling, specific, differentiated and defensible:

◊ **Simple**. It's easily understood by current
  and prospective customers.
◊ **Compelling**. It describes something that is
  interesting or desirable to them.
◊ **Specific**. It captures what your product does,
  not an overly abstract statement of it.
◊ **Differentiated**. It includes something that
  makes it unique among peers.
◊ **Defensible**. It isn't easy for competitors to adopt or copy.

Without clear messaging about what your product does, you leave room for people to make up their own mind and their own messaging. And that's how you end up with five people all failing to describe an elephant, or in your case, try your product.

> "If you don't have your story and messaging right, no amount of money spent on tactics like paid acquisition will work. You'll bring people to your product only to find a message that doesn't resonate. Getting your story straight is crucial to convincing them your product is going to meet their needs."
>
> – MATT (FIRST MARKETING HIRE)

SELLING YOUR PRODUCT

You may be thinking, "Wait a minute. I started my own company because I'm passionate about X, not to become a salesman." This couldn't be further from the truth. As soon as you start your own company, sales needs to be part of the conversation.

But when is the right time to bring in a dedicated sales team? We brought in sales relatively late. In fact, we acquired nearly 2,000 paying customers relying purely on content and word of mouth alone. This isn't unique to Intercom; the role of marketing at SaaS companies is expanding, and is now responsible for phases further down the funnel.

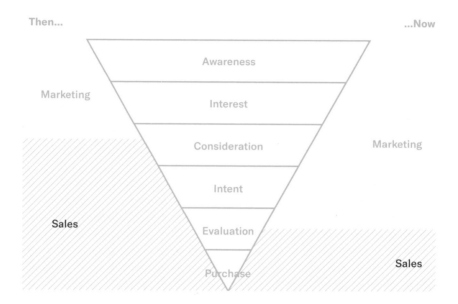

Here's how we segmented the market in the early days of our sales operations. Bear in mind that our sweet spot was selling to other SaaS companies and startups, so you'll need to adapt this for your own unique circumstances.

SELLING TO COMPANIES OF LESS THAN 10 EMPLOYEES

Characteristics:
- ◊ The company consists of founders and engineers
- ◊ They act like consumers because they are spending their own money
- ◊ Money is tight so they do everything on the cheap and build it themselves

Sales strategy:
- ◊ Sell to them like a consumer app: no sales people and make it all self-service
- ◊ Devote money you would have spent on sales to marketing. High-quality content lets you reach a much wider audience than 50 cold calls a day, and you'll know the people coming in are at least slightly interested in your product

SELLING TO COMPANIES OF 11-25 EMPLOYEES

Characteristics:
- ◊ The focus is still on product and engineering
- ◊ They have started to get traction. They might have raised funding, and so are starting to spend other people's money
- ◊ At this size organizations need tools and they tend to get a lot done with a few of them

Sales strategy:
- ◊ It's a great time to get in and grow with a company; they are willing to spend real money on tools
- ◊ You can introduce sales now but most companies at this size prefer self-service because the individuals making decisions are used to doing everything themselves

SELLING TO COMPANIES OF 26-75 EMPLOYEES

Characteristics:
- ◊ Another management layer is introduced and not everyone reports to the CEO
- ◊ As the number of employees grows, so do budgets, process and managers

Sales strategy:
- ◊ You can add a sales team to your company to focus on this size of firm; it's justified by the amount of money they have to spend
- ◊ From a sales perspective, this is often described as the best time to start and grow with a company. It's right before hyper-growth starts

Matching sales to your customer type is invaluable as you grow, when you may be dealing with customers of differing sizes and determining what size companies you should be targeting. Even if you aren't directly involved in the sales process, it can provide a useful look in the mirror if you are working at a startup that's on this kind of growth curve.

EXPLORE MULTIPLE CHANNELS TO FIND THE RIGHT ONE FOR YOUR BUSINESS

Don't think that you'll find a single magical channel that will deliver thousands of users overnight. Exploring many different channels and sources is the only way to find what strategy works best for you. In fact, Airbnb only became the company it is today by going door to door in New York City, recruiting new users and helping existing ones improve their listings. It certainly wasn't from sending cold LinkedIn messages.

How should you think about competitors?

Foreword by Des Traynor, Co-Founder and Chief Strategy Officer

—————

When we started Intercom, we didn't try align ourselves with a particular product category or against a particular competitor. Our competitors became more obvious later, when we started realizing which solutions people were considering alongside ours. But early on, our premise was pretty simple: if you have a web business and you want to talk to your customers you should use Intercom.

Today you might call this category creation, but we weren't going for that at the time. We weren't trying to sell anything other than what we were: a solution to a few problems we knew existed: "Are your customers slipping away? Are they not onboarding correctly? Are they not using all your features?" We aligned ourselves around the problems we knew people had and people bought us for those problems. They didn't buy us because they were shopping around for a product in the support or marketing category.

It helped that we were selling a technology that was innovative: in-app messaging. The early customer conversations usually went like this: "You're the guys that do those in-app messages, right?" or "I saw your product used on ____ and it's something I need too." People weren't comparing Intercom to Zendesk or Marketo. There were no bake-offs or feature battles.

AS YOUR COMPANY GROWS, CUSTOMERS START ASKING ABOUT YOUR COMPETITORS

How does Intercom compare to Zendesk?

Company maturity

How are we different from X?

What's an Intercom?

What our company and products do?

If there were, and if we had employed analysts to plot the competitive landscape, it likely would have been a distraction, if not sent us entirely off course. Today we're quite aware of the products that compete with us, but back then we focused only on the problems we wanted to solve. That's always my advice to new companies as well. Focus on the problem you're solving; worrying about competitors can come later.

All founders can relate to the pressure of launching first. It's a common belief that if your competitor beats you to market, they'll get rich and you'll be dead. But is that really true?

As it turns out, not really. More often than not, being first doesn't matter. According to research by the American Marketing Association, 47% of first-movers fail, compared with 8% of fast followers.

The cost of success is that people will copy you, so if your app takes off, you can bet there will be 20 knockoffs just weeks after you hit the front page of Product Hunt. So how should you deal with the competition? Consider this our guide to moving first, disruption and what that means for your product.

BEING FIRST DOESN'T MATTER

Alan Cooper, father of the Visual Basic programming language, said that being first to market means nothing. Yes, being first offers opportunities which can be exploited as advantages. But those first mover advantages have a short shelf life and eventually need to be replaced with long term strategies.

The three first mover advantages you can gain are technological, defensive or customer. Let's break each one down to see how you can harness it.

1. Maintain a technological head start

If you define a category yourself, you have a potential head start since you're the one trailblazing. You'll have the expert knowledge, analytics and customer feedback that nobody else has, so you should keep that very quiet.

Don't release prototypes, explain how anything works or even broadcast customer feedback. If you do, it gives competitors a head start. Otherwise, they would need to learn all of this themselves, but you've given it to them for free instead.

A great example of how not to do this is Google Glass, which is perplexing if you look at it through this lens. Google chose to throw away all of its advantages by releasing the product in an embryonic phase. It was never officially launched, nor was it developed in secret.

Instead, it was in market, unfinished for anyone to use and for tech bloggers to shower with. If there were any good use cases for the product, competitors discovered them and iterated quickly on better products that fulfilled the same function.

2. Make defensive moves

So you're out-innovating your competitors, but now you need to defend yourself. There are many tactics you could employ to stop competitors from following your exact footsteps, but here are a few examples:

◊ **Secure exclusive partnerships** with core component suppliers, such as paying a supplier large sums to ensure that no one else can use their technology in your industry. e.g when AT&T paid over the odds for exclusive rights to launch the iPhone.

◊ **Kill primary distribution channels** for your competitors, such as block booking advertising with your best performing networks or platforms e.g when Zappos aggressively advertised against shoe manufacturers.

◊ **Win patents** to prevent your technology being directly copied and used in your industry. e.g. Amazon's 1-Click patent.

The key is using your first mover advantage to ensure that it's an advantage for as long as possible – possibly enough to win the market entirely.

3. Lock up the early customers

By locking-in the early adopters – those who are the fastest to adopt new technology, or most influential in the space – it can become impossible for your competition to get a foothold.

This is particularly effective in the formative stages of a new product category, and there are two different ways to do this:

◊ **Bribery:** Simply give away free devices or accounts to noteworthy people, and let them spread the word.
◊ **Long-term contracts:** If you're confident your product is sufficiently desirable, remove mobility of customers with a nice 12- or 18-month contract.

A great example of this is Uber. In the earliest days of Uber, the company took to the ground to give out millions of free coupons to customers, offered heavy discounts to anyone referring their friends and even persuaded its competitors' drivers to switch with cash incentives and appealing car loans (which happened to lock them in for up to two years).

WHAT TO DO ABOUT YOUR FAST FOLLOWERS

If you are first in your market, you alone bear the costs of creating the market. You alone need to convince the world your offering is valid and once you've done that, your fast followers show up.

The copycats have all the advantages. They can copy the best parts of your products, don't make your mistakes and can even use your product to explain their own.

Their weakness? They don't actually know what they're doing, so they have no vision.

ADMIN FEATURES	👤
Reports	📄
Projections	🕐
Distribution	📑
Metrics	〽️
Alerts	⚠️

TOO MUCH STUFF	👤
Reports	📄
No one uses this	🕐
This is broken	📑
Never made sense	〽️
Alerts	⚠️

You look at competitors and think:
"We need to copy all these!"

They look at their product and think:
"We need to remove half of these!"

These fast followers might be able to copy the "what" of your product but never the "why." Their best outcome is a bad copy of your already hurried execution.

One thing to keep in mind is that speed is important. If you're moving forward fast enough, you'll limit these followers to shipping yesterday's ideas tomorrow. The first mover advantage isn't just given to the first product in any category, and it might not exist in your industry yet – it's fought for and earned.

So, with this knowledge, is first mover advantage really quantifiable? According to the Harvard Business Review it's nothing more than a half-truth, and the results vary so wildly that it can't be measured. Sure, if you execute and use it to your advantage it's real, but it's also possible you're first and then your startup dies when something better comes along.

In a product-focused world it varies by category, too. If you look at how Gmail rapidly disrupted email services, but then the category fell stagnant for the following ten years, you'd probably think once a market's been won it's over. But in that time, hundreds of social networks were born, bought, acquired and killed.

The same is true of payment technologies. For almost a decade there was no innovation in payments for businesses or consumers. But suddenly in the last few years, Stripe, Square, Braintree and many others have disrupted the market entirely.

Gmail may have "won" email, but the reality is fairly simple: nothing better has come along since, and sometimes categories can go dormant for a long time before suddenly seeing a jump in innovation.

WHAT ABOUT DISRUPTION?

Almost every startup from every incubator claims to be disruptive, but if you look closely the claim almost always falls apart. There are only two types of disruption: new market disruption and low end disruption.

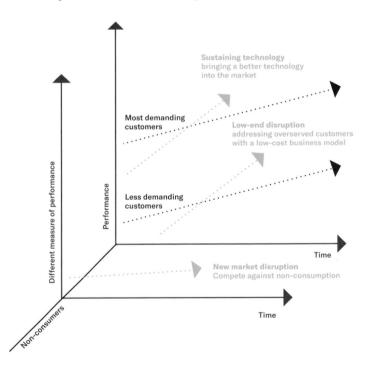

New market disruptions provide a simplifying technology that a whole new set of customers can use. For example, your product is available for customers in a new way. Think Spotify's music service versus buying MP3s on iTunes.

It could be that you're cheaper, available in more countries or an entirely new mechanism of delivery. A good example is Ryanair, the low-cost European airline that created an entirely new market of travellers by offering routes that nobody else did at prices that were on par with trains, buses and even driving. Suddenly air travel was available to millions.

Low end disruption is when a product steals the worst, cheapest customers from the bottom of an existing market by finding a better business model that works with an even lower-cost offering. This opportunity only exists when the market leader is producing products on a higher tier than what the wider market wants or even needs. This doesn't always need to be financial either. For example, it's easier for users to jump on Twitter and make a 140-character tweet than it is to blog, which requires setting up Wordpress and knowing how to get a domain name.

Another example of this is the Flip digital camera which launched in 2007 and stole customers from the digital camera companies – Canon, Nikon and Sony – by being more affordable and easy to use. Bought for $590 million by Cisco in 2009, Flip was the darling of the camera industry and the poster child of low end disruption. What could go wrong?

It turned out there was an even worse video camera at an even lower price point that the public were happy to use: the free camera in smartphones. Two years after its acquisition, Flip got to experience low end disruption itself. It was shut down, and 550 employees were let go.

What's important to take away from this is that disruption can be swift, not slow. Everyone will give you disruption examples like Intel processors or mainframe computers, which realistically took decades to impact the industry, but this isn't always the case.

In an online world where instant global availability is a few clicks away, market adoption can take minutes, not months. Flip's camera only claimed the throne for 18 months before dying. Another great example are sat nav companies Garmin and TomTom. In September 2007 they were worth $38 billion combined. As we discussed in Chapter 1, once the iPhone came along, the sat nav business was decimated.

You might be despairing by this point, because you've realized your business isn't disruptive, but don't. Not all businesses need to be disruptive. It's entirely possible to go head to head with existing businesses and beat them at their own game over time by using better technology, design, product, route to market, etc. This is a proven route to take, but a slightly longer one.

ONLY THE PARANOID SURVIVE

As Andy Grove, Intel's longtime CEO, said, "Success breeds complacency, complacency breeds failure and only the paranoid survive."

Startup founders have to remember that their product is already obsolete because it's out in the world and people are already using it.

That comes with the risk that there's probably a newer, faster way for your customers to get things done in the world. And it doesn't involve you. Even if everything is going great, competitors are emerging. Before you know it, the ground has been torn out from under you – but you might not have even felt it.

It's fun to imagine the sat nav companies were all asleep at the cash register, completely ignoring all these new threats. The reality is that they were probably all watching the iPhone keynote and couldn't believe what they were seeing.

Customers don't wait around for you to innovate. The world will move on, with or without you. What typically happens is that someone puts something out, and the incumbent just says, "Yeah, but who will use that?" And by the time they've decided to fight, it's already a done deal.

Another simple example: SMS text messaging. SMS was a phenomenal technology and was liquid profit for telcos. Then a handful of engineers got together and built WhatsApp. Within two years they'd obliterated the majority of the growth in the most profitable part of telcos.

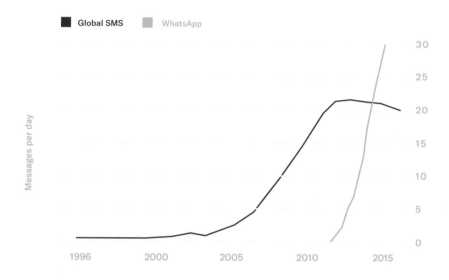

■ Global SMS   ■ WhatsApp

The way this plays out typically is a new threat emerges and the incumbent typically dismisses it as a toy. A few months later when WhatsApp put out a press release saying they had reached 100,000 users the telcos probably laughed.

Then at some point WhatsApp puts out a press release saying, "We have our 100 millionth user," and the telcos think, "Oh." By the time they decide to fight, it's already a done deal, and there's no turning back.

The lesson is that all of these technologies and companies are intertwined. It wasn't clear that a phone would decimate the mapping business, or that software would disrupt telecommunications businesses.

The question you have to consistently ask yourself as new things emerge every day is: "Does this new technology make it in any way cheaper, faster or easier for our customers to make progress in their lives?"

Whenever you see something new, assess whether it makes a difference to your customers, because if it does, they'll start using it – and you'll be left wondering how the ground moved beneath you. The very second you find yourself moving slower than the industry, it's game over.

COMPETITION IS COMPLEX

It's hard to know what's important to focus your attention on, but you should constantly question if someone is outpacing you using superior technology, speed, ease of use or any other factor that could make life better for the people out there using your products.

It's important to decide if it's relevant to your business to try and chase a new area, and risk ending up with a "jack of all trades" product. Ultimately you don't want to be the one caught on camera laughing at something that's about to take the world by storm.

Many people wonder why startup founders are so paranoid. It's because once they've successfully created something that works, they want it to survive long term. So they're constantly worried about what could be around the corner.

What will you measure?

Foreword by Bobby Pinero, Senior Director of Finance & Analytics

————

I came to Intercom right after we closed our Series A funding round. At that point it was just product people at Intercom. I think our Series A investor, Mamoon Hamid from Social Capital, looked around and said it was time to get the house in order from a finance and measurement perspective.

Joining at that early stage, right before we hit one million dollars in Annual Recurring Revenue (ARR), was really insightful. Eoghan and the founders had done a great job setting up the fundamentals, but by bringing in finance and analytics early, we could start to understand deeper questions about the business. We could figure out where that ARR was coming from. How could we think about it moving forward? Why might we need future capital? When might we need it? Who might we want to start hiring?

Getting these questions answered made our later rounds of fundraising easier. Your job while fundraising, whether you're the CEO or the CFO, is to use data to build a case for why your company is going to be X times more valuable than it is today. Then it's up to you to put that data together in a compelling story.

What we're looking for

- $600k convertible note
- 18 months of runway to work on:
  - product market fit
  - customer dev
  - early marketing efforts
  - profitability
- Plan to raise further round in 12-18 months to turn up heat on marketing

Every business is so different. Every business has a different story, is selling to different segments, has different market positioning and has different buyers. For us, it was all about finding the metrics that proved Intercom was on the road to being successful.

Bringing finance and analytics in early also meant we could all get on the same page regarding metrics. One mistake I see at a lot of other early stage startups is that they don't have well-defined sources of truth. People start talking about churn, but what are they really talking about? Are they talking about gross Monthly Recurring Revenue (MRR) churn? Are they talking about net MRR churn? Are they talking about customer churn? Too often, metrics get thrown out, and it's unclear exactly what they mean. It's easy to spend a lot of time arguing about the actual data and numbers instead of figuring out what that data and numbers are telling you.

When you're building a startup, data can be like a warm blanket on a cold night. Data is comforting. It can be trusted. It's black and white with no apparent shades of grey. As Clay Christensen has said, "Many people view numerical data as more trustworthy than qualitative data."

The reality is that data can introduce even more uncertainty into your business if not used correctly. Because humans are deciding what to measure, how to measure and why to measure, almost all data is built on biases and judgement.

That doesn't mean you should ignore data and act on intuition alone. The point is that data is only one lens on your business. What your users are saying is another perspective. What you want to do internally is another. What makes financial sense is another.

For example, if Apple were driven by data, they would have shut down their Genius Bar after years of no activity. If Ryanair were customer driven they'd remove all their sneaky fees and charges. If Zappos were driven by margins, they'd abandon their generous returns policy. They're all just perspectives. Just because data is objective, it doesn't mean that it guides you to the right decision. Just because it's precise, it's not necessarily valuable.

Early stage companies have limited resources in terms of attention, so it's critical to focus on data that's important to them, not necessarily what conventional wisdom tells them to measure. For example, If you're looking to disrupt a well-defined market, then you should know that the success of your company won't be measured by the same metrics used by the big players in the market. Airbnb and the Hilton group have very different definitions of success, but each are valid for their business.

Alternatively if you're establishing a new space, or new type of product, it's nearly impossible to know what metrics you should be optimizing for. Sure you study your signup funnel, optimize your landing page and simplify the onboarding. That's the easy bit. The real challenge is working out how to turn signups into serious long-term customers. The relevant metrics for this only emerge over time. Until then you can pore aimlessly over your dashboards, or as we've always found to be more productive, start talking to customers.

Regardless of your business, you're likely going to want data to help you do two things:

◊ Improve your product
◊ Grow your business

Let's explore these in a little more detail.

DATA TO HELP YOU IMPROVE YOUR PRODUCT

Understanding how people interact with and use your product will help you make better decisions about how to improve it. Sometimes this is about new features, other times it's about the smaller details. For example, did that design tweak to your signup flow have any impact on people dropping out of the funnel?

CUSTOMER FEEDBACK

One of the issues you face as your startup grows and begins to gain traction is that suddenly everyone has opinions about your product. You will drown in them.

But not all customers are the same. All feedback is not equal. This is what one-size-fits-all surveys get wrong. Make sure you're collecting customer feedback from the right sources.

- ◊ If you want to improve your onboarding, talk to this week's sign-ups while the experience is fresh in their mind.
- ◊ If you want to know how your interface scales, talk to the people with hundreds of active projects (or galleries, libraries, etc.).
- ◊ If you want to understand the challenges in getting an entire team to switch to your app, talk to people who have just added their whole team.

Follow these six principles to analyze and understand the type of feedback that is most important to your business:

1. The type of customer giving the feedback matters
Customers who have been loyal the longest have a wealth of experience with your product that makes their opinions particularly valuable. Do you have some customers who only started using your product six months ago but use it heavily? They're likely to have a lot of insightful feedback. Do you have some customers who pay significantly more than others? You may want to factor that in too.

2. Whether it's prompted or unprompted, customer feedback matters

The customer issues that aren't on your radar, that you're completely unaware of, can be the most important things you need to hear. You're more likely to hear those left-field issues via unsolicited feedback or from open ended survey questions rather than, say, a survey with multiple choice answers.

3. The customer's motivations matter

People are generally motivated to provide unsolicited feedback if they have an extreme experience. That's why you see Yelp restaurant reviews clustered around the "amazing" and "appalling" end of the spectrum. But the night your dinner was really average? You're probably not going to bother writing a review because, well, what's the point? It's not a very interesting story is it? When it comes to customer feedback you've probably got a large group in the middle who think your product is "fine". These customers typically stay silent but they could have also have useful feedback for you. If you're smart, you'll find ways to tease it out.

4. Volume matters

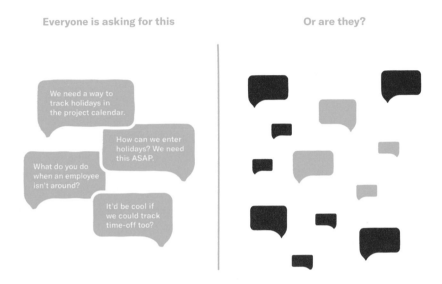

If 80% of your customer feedback in the last month is telling you that the "improvement" you made recently to your core product has broken people's workflow, you should listen up. The overall volume of feedback about a single issue relative to other issues matters. It will also protect you from "fre-cently" bias, where people assume things they hear frequently or recently have the greatest importance.

5. Repetition matters

User issues are often dismissed on the grounds that, "Oh we've heard that for ages". Maybe you're planning to finally address it in a big redesign next year. Or more likely this request has become so repetitive that it's now trite, a sort of dull whine that nobody listens to anymore. Either way, this kind of feedback is really worth listening to. It's an indicator that you haven't got the basics right, and that's something you have to address as a priority rather than ignore.

6. The stakes matter
Some feedback is worth listening to purely because of the severity of the problem the customer is experiencing. This is high stakes feedback. Perhaps you pushed a release that had a security loophole, or your product has accidentally put your customers' privacy at risk. When reviewing customer feedback, try to build a mechanism that alerts you to this very occasional but high stakes feedback so you can take action straightaway.

PRODUCT ANALYTICS
The world of startups is full of "golden rules" about dated metrics like bounce rate, time on site, pages per visit and more. For modern software products, these rules are bullshit. It's not that they're incorrect, it's just that these rules offer information that isn't actionable and doesn't matter to your business. Google's Avinash Kaushik puts it best, "The average conversion rate in the United States of America whether you're selling elephants or iPods, will be 2%".

We've found three metrics to be fundamental to understanding the overall health of a product:

1. **Intent to use:** The actions customers are taking that tell you definitively they intend to use your product e.g. customer has imported custom data.
2. **Activation:** The point when a customer gets real value from your product e.g. customer has invited five teammates in seven days.
3. **Engagement:** How much, how often and how long customers continue to gain value from the product e.g. the number of photos uploaded per user per day.

These metrics mean very different things to different businesses. A $99 B2B SaaS app defines engagement very differently from an ecommerce website. So rather than fixating on what others are measuring, take time to understand which metrics are most important for your business.

DATA TO HELP YOU GROW

When a VC comes knocking with questions about your business, you need to have your house in order. Know the difference between your gross churn and your net churn.

It takes time to identify and understand each of these metrics in the context of your business. More importantly, it takes deep analysis and constant experimentation to understand how you can impact them. You don't want to be considering these metrics for the first time when you get a query about them from a potential investor. Plan accordingly. If you don't already have an analyst on your team, seriously consider hiring one that can own this.

With today's analytics tools, it's easy to measure hundreds, if not thousands of different metrics for your business. Cutting through all the noise to determine the most important or insightful metrics can be quite a challenge. Don't worry, we've got you covered. Here are the most important financial metrics your startup should measure. (It's worth noting this section applies only to SaaS startups. If you're running an ecommerce business, your metrics will likely be different.)

MONTHLY RECURRING REVENUE (MRR) BUILD

Ultimately, your valuation and the amount that you're able to raise will be calculated from a combination of:

- ◊ Your current MRR
- ◊ How quickly you've gotten there
- ◊ The rate at which you're adding to it
- ◊ The rate at which you're losing it

It's as simple as that.

Here's a summary of how you should present this:

METRICS	DEFINITION/CALCULATION
Visits/leads	A count of unique people that find you.
Onboarding funnel	Lay out the conversion steps relevant to your business i.e. submit an email address, take a trial, etc.
New customers & MRR	Monthly Recurring Revenue that started paying during the period in question.
Expansion customers & MRR	Upselling from existing customer base.
Contracted customers & MRR	Downgrades from existing customer base.
Churned customers & MRR	MRR that cancelled this period.
Net new MRR	= New MRR + Expansion MRR - Contraction MRR - Churned MRR
BOP MRR	Beginning of period (BOP) MRR = Last periods End of Period (EOP) MRR
EOP MRR	= BOP MRR + Net New MRR
EOP annual recurring revenue (ARR)	= EOP MRR x12
SaaS quick ratio*	(New MRR + Expansion MRR) / (Contracted MRR + Churned MRR)

You want your SaaS Quick Ratio to be over 4

CUSTOMER RETENTION

MRR retention will make or break the growth of your SaaS business. There's no point filling the bucket if it's full of holes. You need to show retention in a few ways.

◊ **Gross Churn:** Of all the committed revenue you had last period (month/quarter/year), how much walked out the door this period?

◊ **Net Churn**: Of all the committed revenue you had last period, how much walked out the door this period net of upsells?

◊ **Cohort Retention**: Churn metrics as described above are a great snapshot into the business at a point in time. However, it's a blended average of all customers at different points in their lifecycle. Retention by cohort gives you a longitudinal view of how good you are at keeping, upselling and cross-selling any given customer and how that has evolved over time. In other words, for every dollar you earn today, how many dollars do you have six months later, one year later, and so on.

CUSTOMER ACQUISITION

This boils down to how you find and acquire new customers. Ask yourself:

◊ How have traffic/lead sources changed over time and what's driving that? Is it repeatable?

◊ How many unique visitors do you get on a monthly basis, and how many of them are from organic traffic sources versus paid?

You need to prove the economics of your acquisition strategy. It's important to calculate the following for your overall business.

◊ **CAC**: Cost of acquiring a customer

◊ **LTV**: Customer Lifetime Value, or how much revenue a customer is worth over the entire time they are a customer

◊ **Contribution Margin**: Revenue from customer minus variable costs associated with a customer

◊ **Payback period**: The time it takes you to recover your CAC

FINANCIAL STATEMENTS

Have all three financial statements – income statement, balance sheet and cash flow – up to date, as well as a copy of your cap table prepared.

Your income statement will be the most scrutinized. Keys to the income statement include:

Gross Profit Margin

Gross Profit is calculated as Revenue – Cost of Goods Sold (COGS) e.g. hosting, support, infrastructure, etc. Great SaaS companies have healthy GP margins at 70% or above.

Department spend

Lay out all non COGS related spend into three buckets:

Research and Development (R&D)

Sales and Marketing (S&M)

General and Administrative (G&A)

The proportions of each will tell the story of where you've invested to build your business.

Operating income or loss

The calculation here is:

Revenue – COGS – R&D – S&M – G&A

Investors want to see how much you burn on a monthly basis and how many months remain with the cash you have in the bank.

PROJECTIONS

While most investors take your rosy projections with a grain of salt, they still want to understand how you're planning for the future. A detailed projection for the next 12 months with high level assumptions applied to the next two to three years is a good place to start. You want to project both your MRR build and your income statement.

Be prepared to talk through the assumptions used to build out these projections. These assumptions should be things that you're able to point to with confidence, particularly the closer they are on the horizon. Also important to note: the projections you share in this situation will most likely be what you're measured against should the deal close.

DON'T BRING A MEASURING TAPE TO A GUNFIGHT

The final piece of advice here is to make sure data doesn't become a false god. Data can be a powerful tool for any startup, but a lot of times it tells a story of what happened in the past, not necessarily what will happen in the future. If you simply rely on data, it can end up bringing you to a local maximum rather than allowing you to hit your full potential. So you iterate and optimize in favor of taking big bets, and never take the steps required to get you out of that local maximum.

The highest rewards come from the biggest risks. Sometimes you need to be willing to say "We believe in this, fuck what the data says". That's when things gets exciting.

CHAPTER NINE

How will you grow?

Foreword by Ben McRedmond, Senior Director of Growth

———

Two years into Intercom's life as a company, we didn't have a marketing team or a sales team. The only marketing we had done was around content, which has always been really important to us. Growth was going up and to the right, but we asked ourselves: What if our growth stops? We'd built this machine that we had very little control over.

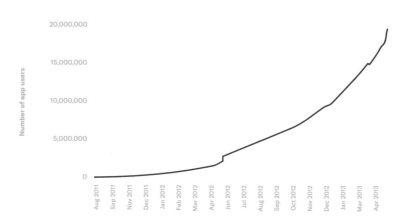

Approaching 20m end users, May 4, 2013

The question we faced was how to be deliberate about our growth. We were getting more and more customers, but nobody was thinking about how to convert customers, how to get them setup, etc. That's how the growth team started at Intercom: an attempt to be intentional about how we were growing.

We probably could have built a team earlier, but we were conscious of the fact that growth tactics can be a distraction if you focus on them before you've found product-market fit. The greatest products will always have some sort of natural growth early on.

That's not to say that the customers just come – they certainly don't. But no amount of growth tactics can grow a product that has yet to find product-market fit. It can bring you short term success, but you'll hit a ceiling sooner or later. You need to validate your product first, and once you've successfully done that, then you can start a growth team.

Many of our early tactics were based on opinions and intuition, rather than on quantitative data. In fact, a common mistake other startups make in the early days is relying too much on quantitative data.

If you're Facebook, and you have several hundred million users, you can test something in minutes or hours. But a startup with a few hundred users could take 12 weeks to get useful data. Our growth tactics were simply our opinion about how software should be built, rather than looking at what other companies were doing.

We looked for plenty of inspiration outside software. What's the purchase experience in your local coffee shop like? If you're buying an Apple product in an Apple store, what happens before, during, and after you buy a product? We've always used real world examples to inform how we sell Intercom.

Looking outside software is a good reminder that there's no such thing as a growth playbook. It drives me crazy when I see lists of "The Top 10 Growth Tactics". There's no secret recipe to success, and basically anyone who is successful has found their own path.

How to grow your startup is one of the questions founders must address in the early stages of starting a company. Growth is the lifeblood of startups, and it's what differentiates Snapchat from the coffee house on the corner – it's exponential.

The majority of advice out there is based around the following formula:

1. Build a product
2. Release a product
3. Growth hack your way to success

Smells like bullshit, or at least some sort of "get rich quick" scheme, right? The Faustian bargain of the internet is that at any time you like, you can swap your credibility for attention. It's not hard to elevate the profile of your product, but ensuring it's for the right reasons is a different challenge.

FOCUS ON THE RIGHT METRICS

One of the easiest mistakes to make when growing a company is focusing on the wrong metric for delivering growth. When someone in the company decides that "accounts created" is the metric for success, for example, the team works out ways to hack that number. Over time people lose sight of what's actually important for the business, and the entire company veers in the wrong direction.

Let's say you hire an analytics consultancy for your project management app. They'll dig into your data and come out with a metric like this: "Users who have invited two or more teammates and posted three updates will upgrade to convert to paying users."

Your "growth hacker" hears this and thinks, "Let's get everyone doing this!" So, you put a big button in the app that forces every user to invite two teammates, create a project and post three messages before they can do anything else.

What happens? Well, users click the button, metrics go up...and upgrades don't follow. Ultimately, lots of things correlate with your users upgrading, but trying to force that trigger doesn't actually do anything. If it did, fires would spontaneously break out near groups of firemen.

Tricking your users in order to hit your metrics causes long term, if not permanent, damage. Any growth you see will be artificial. Trying to get potential customers to do something prematurely – be it creating an account, tweeting or just completing a task – has a similar effect. They're likely to try it once, leave, and never even remember you exist.

> "Focus on high-effort, high-impact work. It's very easy for growth teams to gravitate towards easy, small tweaks that don't have that much impact. We did a bunch small things early on, but none of it paid off a huge amount in anything but the very immediate short term. The things that have had the biggest impact have been the high effort, strategic work."
>
> – BEN (FIRST HIRE)

Homejoy was a good example of why you need to focus on the right metrics. Despite touting "enormous top-of-funnel growth curves" in the press, seemingly out of nowhere, the house cleaning service closed completely, even with $40 million in the bank.

It turns out that even though that top-level growth number looked really good for a while, it wasn't real growth, because none of those users stuck around after the introductory offer expired. As founders, it's easy to choose a vanity metric. We usually choose the biggest number to get press coverage, but it tends to be meaningless, like views, downloads or registrations. Brian Balfour, CEO of Reforge, calls it the wheel of meaningless growth.

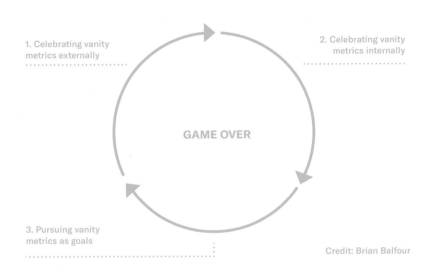

WHEEL OF MEANINGLESS GROWTH

1. Celebrating vanity metrics externally

2. Celebrating vanity metrics internally

GAME OVER

3. Pursuing vanity metrics as goals

Credit: Brian Balfour

When you put that number in the press, you're celebrating it externally and it becomes a trap. Now you have to keep coming up with a bigger and bigger version of that number, so that you're following it into oblivion before you even realize it.

If you choose a vanity metric, you set your entire company up to pursue one thing: growing that number at all costs. Instead of delivering real value for your users, your team is laser-focused on doing anything that grows that number, likely at a cost to the experience of the people actually using your product.

A great example of this exact problem is Twitter. For years, Twitter has been fixated on a single metric: monthly active users. It defined it early on as a number for success, following in Facebook's footsteps, and now that it's a public company, that's all investors care about.

As a result, Twitter has spent the better part of the last three years doing everything it can to inflate that number, at the peril of its 313 million existing users. Instead of making Twitter better for the people who are already using it, it alienated its core user base by introducing features designed to help beginners across the board – like hiding @mentions for everyone – dumbing down the proposition for more experienced users.

> "Growth teams focus way too much on optimization early on. Optimizing implies that your starting point is correct. But every startup inherits things that don't really make sense or weren't really thought through. The much more important thing is to figure out the absolute best experience for new customers and build that from scratch."
>
> – BEN (FIRST HIRE)

Because Twitter focused on that growth metric so early on, it's committed to growing it, and when it doesn't, the stock market punishes the company. It defined its own success by that number, and now it's beholden to it for the long term.

GROWTH IS EVERYONE'S JOB

Paul Graham in his canonical essay, *Startup = Growth*, described a startup like so:

"A startup is a company designed to grow fast. Being newly founded does not in itself make a company a startup. Nor is it necessary for a startup to work on technology, or take venture funding, or have some sort of exit."

By this definition, everyone in a startup is, or should be, working on growth. Engineering teams don't exist to write code. Engineering teams exist to apply science to build products to grow the company. Marketing teams don't exist to make landing pages. Marketing teams exist to communicate the value of a product, service or brand to grow the company.

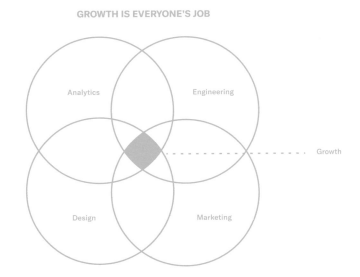

GROWTH IS EVERYONE'S JOB

The only difference between product teams and marketing teams at a startup is that one is focused on long term growth, and the other is focused on immediately measurable growth. When a product team releases a feature, they don't expect signups or revenue to jump overnight. But when a marketing team starts a new campaign, immediate results are expected.

Ultimately, both teams work on growth. The biggest difference is the period in which results can be measured. For near term growth oriented product teams (often called "growth teams") and marketing teams, focusing on immediately measurable results should not translate to focusing on trivial changes – the sizes of the changes you're willing to make will directly correlate with the size of your returns.

In simpler terms: a billion dollar company was never built from better button colors.

GROWTH COMES FROM HIGH-EFFORT, HIGH-IMPACT WORK

The key for any businesses is learning to focus on the hard stuff. We're talking about the high-effort, but high-impact work. Hunter Walk, Partner at Homebrew VC, taught us that most people automatically opt for the low-effort work, which is a little like snacking.

Walk said that you can eat snacks when you're hungry and it helps, but if you only ever ate snacks you'd eventually die.

If you know something is better and it's hard to implement, you don't need to A/B test it. Too many startups slow down their roadmaps at the start because they're overly concerned with measuring every single detail. At some point you might be a Facebook or a Twitter and you can measure things quickly. In that case do it, but don't obsess over it.

For example, when we redesigned our signup flow in the early days of Intercom, there was very little numerical justification up front for doing so. It took us six months to complete, but it was one of the most impactful changes for our business. If we were obsessing over numbers it might not have ever happened.

To avoid the pitfalls of smaller, "snack" metrics, it's important to pair every single metric with an appropriate counter metric: signups with activations, new paid customers with churn or new paid customers with total revenue. This achieves two things:

1. It recognizes that your product is a system of metrics, highlighting that focusing on any metric in isolation is incorrect.
2. By recognizing and forcing focus on the system, it encourages a more holistic approach to growth.

Encouraging this kind of holistic approach naturally moves you away from trivial button colors or headline tweaking. It also leads you to some more impactful questions that will help you grow:

1. Are you describing your product in the same language and terms that prospective customers use to articulate their problems? If questions are where answers fit, this is critical to prospective customers finding a place for your product in their head.
2. When did you last sign up for your product? Does anyone in your company own the signup flows? You'll likely be embarrassed by the assumptions you made early on, and quite possibly no one has worked on signup since.
3. How do you teach customers about your product? Are you helping them solve their problems? Or are you merely describing the mechanics of your product? ("The message button is over there, good luck!").

These are the types of questions from which real, sustainable growth originates. It's not as easy as changing a button color and hoping for 80% more conversions. But then again, nobody said growing a startup was easy.

August 2011 | *Intercom's four founders in San Francisco on the day Intercom was incorporated*

2013 | *Company hike in Ireland*

June 2013 | *Paul Adams deep in planning mode*

May 2012 | *All of Intercom in Dublin*

April 2014 | *Toast at the company all hands*

Des, Ben, Ciaran, Darragh and David

April 2014 | *The entire company with our Series A & B investors, Mamoon and Ethan (seated, center)*

The marketing team take a snack break with Eoghan